pieminister

* a pie for all seasons *

Tristan Hogg and Jon Simon

BANTAM PRESS

LONDON · TORONTO · SYDNEY · AUCKLAND · JOHANNESBURG

TRANSWORLD PUBLISHERS
61–63 Uxbridge Road, London W5 5SA
A Random House Group Company
www.transworldbooks.co.uk

First published in Great Britain
in 2011 by Bantam Press
an imprint of Transworld Publishers

A CIP catalogue record for this book
is available from the British Library.

ISBN 9780593068052

Addresses for Random House Group Ltd companies outside the UK can be
found at: www.randomhouse.co.uk
The Random House Group Ltd Reg. No. 954009

The Random House Group Ltd supports the Forest Stewardship Council
(FSC), the leading international forest-certification organization. All our
titles that are printed on Greenpeace-approved FSC-certified paper carry
the FSC logo. Our paper procurement policy can be found at
www.rbooks.co.uk/environment

Design A-Side Studio
Photography James Bowden
Additional photography Lincoln Jefferson and Caroline Vail
Food styling Lincoln Jefferson
Illustrations and cover design Ryan Thomas
Recipe editing and testing Jane Middleton

This book was created by harris + wilson *and* pieminister

Typeset in Egizio & Albert
Printed and bound in Great Britain by Butler Tanner & Dennis Ltd, Frome

10 9 8 7 6 5 4 3 2 1

contents

introduction

We love pies, we've always loved pies! Over the years we've cooked and eaten thousands of them. Not surprisingly we have learnt a lot about pies. We have been called leaders of the pie revolution, pie-oneers, the upper crust of pie-makers and numerous other dreadful puns. People have handed us recipes in the street, sent us poems about pies and presented us with pies to try. We have talked about very little else for the past eight years.

We now think it's our duty to share all our knowledge with you. We have pulled in lots of favours and flavours from friends, family, suppliers and the pieminister team to bring you a book filled with great recipes. We went shooting in Devon, cheese-making in Somerset, foraging and surfing in Cornwall, fishing in Dorset and partying in Bristol – all in the name of pie!

This was not just for our own selfish gratification, but for the good of all. Our aim has been to elevate pies to where they truly belong: the food of the gods!

There is a (sad) misconception that pies are simply a winter dish, comfort food for cold and stormy nights. In our book we have set out to prove this theory wrong. We have made pies that are filled with seasonal ingredients, great for summer parties, eating on the beach, spring suppers and autumn lunches. Small ones, big ones, breakfast ones, fruit ones, family ones and ones that make you go oooooh! We've included baking and pastry tips (you'll find these at the beginning of the book) and accompaniments to go with pies (at the end of the book). To see you through the seasons, there are also features on everything from tips on how to survive a festival to Christmas party games.

Put simply, a pie is a good filling with some kind of casing – a bottom or a top, or both. And the covering doesn't have to be pastry, of course. It can be mash, crumble, grated cheese, a breadcrumb mix . . . There are no real rules when making pies. We've included rolls, strudels, tarts, crumbles and turnovers.

Have fun, try our stuff, try your own stuff and try your friends' stuff, and enjoy the fact that you are keeping the ancient tradition of pie-making alive. We hope you enjoy using this book as much as we have enjoyed making it.

Jon and Tristan

pieminister cabinet: Jon (left) and Tristan (right)

a brief history of pieminister

We met as teenagers in the early 1990s. After a first meeting at Tristan's home (Jon was dating Tristan's sister at the time) we went on to become great friends. Jon owned a bar in London and Tristan came to work there as a chef at the tender age of 18. We had fun and, between us, we made the bar a thriving success – mostly down to the groundbreaking menu. We decided that we should set up in business together some day.

Pies were on the agenda. Jon had travelled to Australia a few years before and stumbled across Harry's Café de Wheels in Woolloomooloo, Sydney, a mecca for all food lovers, celebrities, cool kids and anyone who knows anything about pies (see page 100). After devouring their famous 'tiger pie' (beef pie with mash, mushy peas and gravy), he realized pretty quickly that this would be a great concept in the UK.

A few years later Tristan was headhunted to work as a chef with touring bands. He became 'a chef to the stars', cooking for giants such as the Rolling Stones, Pet Shop Boys and Robbie Williams. After his stint working for these legends, Tristan moved to Australia to sunbathe, surf and learn from the Antipodeans the art of cooking and, more importantly, research pies in greater depth. It was there, on Bondi Beach, while eating a Thai chicken pie, that the pieminister name was born.

Tristan returned from Australia full of excitement. Armed with the name for our new venture, we started pieminister.

We set about perfecting the first range of pies from the basement of Tristan's family home in the heart of Bristol. We tested more than 200 recipes before coming up with what we thought was the best line-up since the 1966 World Cup. Our aim was simple – to make the best pies we possibly could. They had to contain only fresh, responsibly sourced, free-range and natural ingredients gathered from as close to our kitchen as possible.

We started sourcing our beef and pork from local farms. We found a great free-range chicken supplier, used local dairies for our milk and free-range eggs and discovered a beautiful mill close by that made award-winning flour. We did our best to work with the seasons so that vegetables, fruit, nuts and herbs gave our range a fantastic variety of flavours throughout the year. Later, when we started doing fish pies, we made sure to use only sustainable fish.

Soon after the first pieminister pie was created in June 2003, we set up a pie shop in Bristol – with a kitchen and a junior minister. Tristan rolled, baked and cooked while Jon tended the shop and wholesale business.

In 2004, not long after the launch of the Bristol shop, we were given the opportunity to trade at the Glastonbury festival and invited to be the only pie stall at the highly acclaimed Borough Market in London. This was just the break we needed. Today, our pies are sold at some of the best music festivals, delis, food halls, farmers' markets and pubs as well as in pieminister cafés scattered around the country.

Now we've written a book telling you all our secrets . . . don't tell anyone!

pastry

All our pastry recipes make around 650–850g, which ensures in most cases that you will have enough to cover your pie generously, with some to spare. If you have some left over after making your pie, fear not – it will keep in the fridge, well wrapped, for a good three days, or can be frozen for future use. Alternatively, you could make nice goodies such as jam tarts or cheese straws (see page 16).

Don't be afraid to make mistakes. Pastry will behave better if it doesn't detect worry in your hands. Pretend to be the boss even if you're scared of your suet crust. And have fun . . .

shortcrust pastry

This sturdy pastry is straightforward to make and simple to use. The proportions are half fat to flour, with enough water added to bind the pastry together. If you want to turn this into a sweet pastry (that isn't too sweet), add 4 tbsp of caster sugar.

Makes about 660g
400g plain flour
a pinch of salt
200g butter, cut into small cubes
about 4 tbsp cold water

Sift the flour into a bowl and add the salt. Add the cubes of butter and rub them into the flour with your fingertips until the mixture looks like breadcrumbs. Gradually stir in enough cold water to make a pliable but fairly firm dough. Knead lightly for 30 seconds or so until smooth, then wrap in clingfilm and chill for at least 30 minutes before use.

rough puff pastry

Compared to its more temperamental sibling, puff pastry, rough puff is pretty straightforward to make. It's a great choice for rich, sumptuous pies. It's very important here that the butter is cold and you don't rub it in, as you really want little pockets of butter . . . remember, butter pockets, not butter fingers!

It's not really practical to make rough puff in a smaller quantity than the one given here, so for some recipes you may have quite a lot left over. Either wrap it well and freeze for another time, or use it in one of the ways suggested on page 16.

Makes about 650g
250g plain flour
a pinch of salt
250g cold butter, cut into 1cm cubes
150ml very cold water
1 tsp lemon juice

Put the flour and salt into a bowl and add the cubes of butter. Mix the water with the lemon juice, then add about three-quarters of it to the flour mixture. Stir briefly until everything comes together into a rough, shaggy dough, adding the remaining water if necessary. Place the dough on a floured board, press it into a square, then roll it out into a long rectangle about 8mm thick. Don't turn the pastry while you are rolling, but be sure to lift it up and flour underneath if it begins to stick.

Fold up the bottom third of the pastry, then fold down the top third, like folding a letter. Give it a quarter turn and roll it out again – it's best to work quickly and lightly so the butter doesn't warm up too much. Fold in three again, wrap in clingfilm and chill for 20 minutes. Repeat the rolling and folding twice, then wrap again and chill thoroughly before using.

suet pastry

This is the quickest pastry of all to make, and extremely simple – the only thing to watch out for is to avoid adding too much water. Although it's associated with steamed puddings, suet pastry also works really well in baked pies. It has to be made by hand or in a mixer with a dough hook. If you tried to do it in a food processor, the suet would be chopped up finely, which would render it unsuety. The whole point of this pastry is the little melty gems of suet, which give it its unique texture and slight flakiness.

Suet is a great pastry to use if you want to include flavourings, such as rosemary, chopped anchovy, cracked black pepper or grated cheese. Because it's rolled slightly thicker than most pastries, the additions won't tear it.

You can use packet suet, either meat or vegetarian, or buy proper old-fashioned beef suet from a butcher. This will have to be put in the freezer before use and then grated into a little flour so the pieces stay separate. It might seem like a lot of trouble but the flavour is fantastic. Beef suet comes from around the kidneys of the animal and is more sustainable than most vegetable suet, which is made from palm oil, with all the environmental implications that has.

Makes about 750g
400g plain flour
a pinch of salt
200g suet
about 120–150ml milk

Put the flour and salt into a bowl and stir in the suet. Gradually stir in enough milk to make a fairly stiff dough – be sure to add it very slowly or you might find the mixture has suddenly become saturated. If this does happen, mix in a little extra flour. Turn the pastry out on to a lightly floured board and knead for a couple of minutes, until smooth – you can treat this pastry more firmly than ones made with butter. Wrap in clingfilm and chill for about 30 minutes before use.

soured cream pastry

This pastry is wonderful to work with. The cream makes it smooth, tender and melt-in-the-mouth, and provides sheen when cooked. It also makes a great base for spices, herbs or citrus zest if you want a flavoured pastry.

Makes about 850g
500g plain flour
a pinch of salt
250g butter, cut into small cubes
90–100ml soured cream

Sift the flour into a bowl and add the salt and butter. Rub the butter into the flour with your fingertips until the mixture looks like breadcrumbs, then stir in enough soured cream to bring it together into a dough. Wrap in clingfilm and chill for about 30 minutes before use.

hot water crust pastry

This pastry is used for making 'cold-eating' raised pies, such as pork pies. It does what it says on the tin: you add hot water to the mix to make a really fun-to-work-with, malleable dough, which you pull up around the filling by hand. A word of warning: do not place this pastry in the fridge or allow it to cool; use it right away or it will be a nightmare trying to get it to work.

Makes about 850g
450g plain flour
2 tsp caster sugar
1 free-range egg, lightly beaten
200ml water
60g butter, cut into cubes
100g lard, cut into cubes

Mix the flour and sugar together in a bowl. Make a well in the centre, pour in the egg and cover with a little of the flour. Put the water, butter and lard in a saucepan and heat gently until the fat has melted and the water is just at boiling point. Slowly pour this mixture into the flour, stirring with a table knife until it forms a dough. Knead the pastry lightly until smooth (perhaps with some rubber gloves on if it's very hot), then use straight away, while it's soft and pliable.

sweet pastry

This pastry is based on the dough for sablé biscuits, a kind of shortbread. *Sablé* is the French word for sandy, which refers to their soft, crumbly texture. If you have any leftover pastry, either freeze it or, better still, make it into little biscuits (see page 16).

As this pastry is so rich, it can be a little tricky to handle, so do make sure you chill it thoroughly before rolling. If it tears when you are lining the tin, don't fret; just patch it with a bit of pastry. Despite everything, this pastry really is worth the work.

If it all sounds too scary, then use the shortcrust with added sugar on page 10. Sissy!

Makes about 700g
250g softened unsalted butter
125g icing sugar, sifted
1 tbsp whipping cream
1 free-range egg yolk
350g plain flour, sifted

Using an electric mixer if you have one, cream the butter until light and fluffy. Beat in the icing sugar, then mix in the cream and egg yolk. Finally, mix in the flour on a low speed until just combined. Turn out on to a floured surface and knead lightly for a few seconds until smooth. Shape into a disc, wrap in clingfilm and chill for at least 4 hours.

puff pastry

Making puff pastry is quite tricky, so we recommend that you buy it. The shop-bought stuff is pretty good these days, especially the ones made with butter, and you can also get very good organic ones. Where we have specified the use of puff (as opposed to rough puff) in a recipe, do use it, as we are looking for 'lift', which you just won't get otherwise.

filo pastry

Tricky to make, so we would expect you to buy this – unless you really have lots of time, in which case refer to a good Greek cookbook or, if you're Greek, ask your grandmother.

crust lust & other notes

Crust lust is the feeling you get when you take a wonderful pie out of the oven that has been prepared using your own pastry. Making your own is so satisfying, quick to do and hugely delicious. It's important to get your pastry-making right, as it's half your pie, but it's by no means magic. Just follow the recipes we have given, use a little patience and intuition – with practice, you will get to know when the pastry feels right – and an amazing crust will unleash itself upon your serving table. Having said that, don't be deterred from making a pie if you really don't have the time or inclination to knock up your own pastry. Some of the ones you can buy are really quite good and we certainly wouldn't disown you if you made use of them occasionally.

So, a few tips to get you started.

hands

People talk about everything needing to be very cold for pastry-making, including your hands, and it does help, as it means the fat is less likely to become greasy. So do what you can to keep the temperature down – if you have warm hands, a good tip is to hold them under cold running water for a few seconds, then pat dry. Don't get too hung up on this, however, as there are more important quality-defining factors than the temperature of your hands. Some recipes recommend using chilled butter but, given the choice, we would work with slightly softer butter over freezing butter any day. You can start the shortcrust and soured cream pastries off in a food processor, which helps prevent them getting too warm: just whiz the flour and fat together, then tip into a bowl and stir in the liquid.

use yummy fats

None of the recipes in this book uses margarine. Instead they all rely on the good old-fashioned stuff, like butter, lard and suet. The pastry will taste 10 times better for using natural fats such as these. If you use vegetable rather than beef suet, you might like to look for one containing non-hydrogenated fat.

liquid

The quantity of liquid given in the pastry recipes can only be a rough guide, as there are so many factors that will determine how much liquid you need – the type of flour you use and the temperature, for example. The best thing to do is to mix about two-thirds of the liquid into the dry ingredients and then add the rest a little at a time until you have a nice, pliable but non-sticky consistency . . . it's hard to explain, but you'll know when you've got it right as your pastry will be easy to work with.

more liquid . . .

Besides water, we sometimes use milk, soured cream or egg yolks. All of these fatty liquids add to the richness of the pastry, making it more tender and velvety.

egg wash

We always use free-range eggs for glazing a pie, as it gives a great sheen. Some people even double-glaze a pie for a super-glossy top – once before cooking and again just as it comes out of the oven piping hot. Cream also works well as a glaze.

relax!

Give your pastry a break. If you'd been manhandled and kneaded for 15 minutes or so, you would require a break and so does pastry. Leave it to rest, wrapped in clingfilm in the fridge, for at least 30 minutes before using. We always pat our pastry into the shape we want to roll it out in before chilling it, so that it rolls neatly when taken out of the fridge. If it's too firm to roll, leave it at room temperature for about 30 minutes first.

rolling your pastry (after it has relaxed)

Get yourself a decent rolling pin, if you are not already the proud owner of one. Lightly flour a work surface and the rolling pin itself. With your hands at either end of the rolling pin, roll out the pastry gently and with even weight across it so that it flattens evenly. Lift it up every few rolls, flouring very lightly underneath if necessary, and give it a quarter turn. As the pastry gets larger, you will have to lift it up on the rolling pin rather than in your hands, so it doesn't break. Be calm and gentle while rolling, to help ensure you don't overstretch the pastry, which could make it tough.

lining a pie dish

Lift up the rolled-out pastry on the rolling pin, wrapping it round loosely if necessary, then hold it over the centre of the pie dish and unroll it into the dish. Lightly press it into the corners with your fingertips, making sure you don't stretch the pastry. Trim off the excess with a sharp knife or, if you are using a dish without a rim, such as a flan tin, just run the rolling pin lightly over the top to cut off the excess. Chill briefly before filling or baking blind; this helps prevent shrinkage in the oven.

If you are lining a deep pie tin or a pudding basin, cut a small triangle out of one side of the pastry after rolling, so you don't get lots of folds when you put it in the dish.

making a pastry lid

Press the trimmings together if necessary and roll them out again as above. Lightly brush the edges of the pastry lining the dish with beaten egg (or brush the rim of the dish with egg if you are making a single-crust pie), then pick up the sheet of pastry on the rolling pin and unroll it over the pie. Trim off the excess with a knife and press the pastry edges together to seal – or just press the pastry on to the egg-washed rim of the dish for a single-crust pie. You need to make a hole in the centre of the pie to let the steam out, but a ripped hole is better than a neatly cut hole, which tends to close up in the oven.

blackbirds and other funnels

These support the top crust, thus helping prevent it becoming soggy, and also help to avoid 'boil out' – which, as the name suggests, is when the filling boils out across the top of your pie.

crimping

This ensures the pastry edges stay firmly sealed during baking. Crimping is also your trademark finish. Some people like to be neat, others take a messier, more rustic approach, so have a play around and see what works for you. It can be as simple as pinching the pastry with your thumb and forefinger all around the edge of the pie, or you can do a more involved design. Be firm but fair when crimping – for a crimp to hold throughout baking, it needs to be shown who's boss beforehand. Make your crimps deeper than you think they need to be without squeezing the filling out. When using two different pastries for the base and lid, leave the pie to stand for about 10 minutes after crimping to allow the pastry top to make friends and bind with the base.

decorating

This is a fun way of using up little scraps of leftover pastry and giving your pie personality. But don't go overboard: too much and you will end up with an uncooked lid due to the double thickness of the pastry. Glaze the pastry lid all over with beaten egg before applying the decorations, then glaze the decorations. We use sprinkles a lot at pieminister, too. Black pepper, herbs, nuts, or whatever you like all look great sprinkled over a pie crust before baking.

cool mix

Unless you are in a real rush and are working very fast, we recommend letting cooked fillings cool before using them.

If it's convenient, you could make the filling the day before and keep it in the fridge overnight. Adding the filling to the pie cold will help prevent the onset of 'soggy bottom' (see below) and 'boil out' (see blackbirds and other funnels, above).

baking blind

Mostly an exercise reserved for tarts and quiches – and quiche is not for this book. However, on the odd occasion here we have opted to bake blind a tart with a fairly liquid filling, or a filling that needs baking at a different temperature from the pastry, or that doesn't need baking at all. You will need some baking parchment or greaseproof paper and ceramic baking beans (available from kitchen shops) or uncooked rice, beans or lentils – these prevent the pastry base rising up and also stop the sides melting down the edge of the tin when the pastry is heating up. Line the uncooked pastry case with the paper, making sure it comes up above the side of the tin, then fill with the beans or rice and bake as instructed in the recipe.

soggy bottom

You get this with bottom-crust pies for a number of reasons: if you don't bake blind when required (see above); if the filling is too liquid or is added while it's hot; if your oven is not hot enough; or if you bake a pie in anything but a metal dish. Putting the pie dish on a hot baking sheet in the oven will help give a crisp pastry base. Always use cooked rather than raw fruit for pies with a bottom crust, otherwise the juices will make the pastry soggy. In some recipes we have used just a pastry lid. This saves time and still tastes mighty good, although a purist might be inclined to tell you off.

'bake off'

If the pie starts to colour too much on top before the filling is thoroughly heated through, then just cover it with foil and move it to the bottom of the oven. The same goes for baking blind if the pastry sides are cooking much faster than the base.

dishes

The right dish is mighty important when making pies. For bottom-crust pies, always go for something metal, to make sure the base cooks properly. You can buy round or rectangular metal pie plates and dishes in various sizes, or you could use a greased deep baking tray or enamel dish. Enamel is a pieminister favourite: it's cheap, comes in lots of different sizes and looks good as well.

You can also use a metal-handled frying pan (i.e. one that can safely go in the oven) or a Le Creuset casserole dish. Earthenware dishes are fine for pies that only have a top crust. Sometimes we don't use a dish at all: we make a pie that just sits on a baking tray. For tarts, a loose-bottomed tin is the one to go for. If you're making a steamed pud, then a good old-fashioned pudding basin is best.

Then you have the filling to think about. In general, it's best not to spread it too thin. Don't overfill your pies either – leave about a centimetre of headspace, so you can seal the pastry lid to the edges.

If you want to know how much filling your dish holds, you can measure its volume by pouring water into it from a measuring jug. Here are the approximate volumes for standard dishes:

- Individual pie dish = approximately 350ml
- 4-person dish = approximately 1.5 litres
- 6-person dish = approximately 2 litres
- 8-person dish = approximately 2.8 litres

In most of the recipes, we haven't specified an exact size for the dish – this is to allow you to use whatever you have to hand. If you find you have some filling left over, then never mind, just make another small pie, or freeze it, or eat it as a casserole in the case of a cooked meat filling.

storage and shelf life

Pies keep in the fridge for a good few days and most of them freeze very well too; just defrost thoroughly before reheating.

using up pastry trimmings

cheese straws

Puff and rough puff are good for these but you can also use shortcrust or soured cream pastry. Press the pastry trimmings together, roll them out to about 3mm thick, then cut into 5cm-wide strips. Brush with beaten egg and scatter generously with grated Cheddar or crumbled Stilton cheese. If you like, you can twist them by picking them up and gently turning the ends to give a spiral. Place on a greased baking sheet and bake at 180°C/350°F/gas mark 4 for 10–15 minutes, until golden.

sablé biscuits

Press together sweet pastry trimmings, roll them out to about 4mm thick and then cut out shapes with a pastry cutter. Place on a greased baking sheet, brush with beaten egg and bake at 180°C/350°F/gas mark 4 for 8–10 minutes, until pale golden. Then sit down with a nice cup of tea and the paper and munch away.

jam tarts

Use shortcrust, sweet pastry, rough puff or puff for these. Roll out the pastry to about 3mm thick, cut out rounds with a pastry cutter and use to line a bun tray. Put a little jam (or lemon curd or even marmalade) in each one and bake at 180°C/350°F/gas mark 4 for 6–8 minutes, until the pastry edges are golden. Be careful not to overfill them or they will bubble over in the oven and you will have a horrible, molten mess. A good tip is to put just a small teaspoonful of jam in each tart, then top them up after baking.

turnovers

You can use any pastry to make a turnover and they are good with both savoury and sweet fillings: try leftover pie filling; grated cheese and cooked onions (or other vegetables); lightly cooked fruit such as apples, gooseberries or rhubarb; a handful of fresh berries, or even jam.

Roll out the leftover pastry to about 3mm thick and cut out circles 12–15cm in diameter. Place the filling to one side of each pastry circle, brush the pastry edges with beaten egg, then fold over to cover the filling. Seal well – turnovers are where you can get really creative with your crimping – brush all over with beaten egg, then place on a baking sheet and bake at 180°C/350°F/gas mark 4 for about 20 minutes, until the pastry is golden brown and the filling is piping hot.

bye-laws & pie-laws

- All the meaty, casserole-type fillings in this book can be cooked in the oven at 180°C/350°F/gas mark 4 if that's more convenient, rather than simmered on the stove. This has the advantage that you don't have to keep checking the filling to make sure it's not sticking or drying out.

- Don't feel you have to keep exactly to the recipe when shaping pies. Use whatever dish you have available, and be creative when it comes to decorating the pastry.

- We like to mix the pastries in a pie – for example, a shortcrust base and a suet top. But if you prefer, you can stick to one kind.

- A really good pie has a filling that can be eaten on its own. Many of our savoury pies use a well-flavoured casserole as a filling.

- Most pie fillings can be made well in advance and kept in the fridge, then covered with pastry and baked when you need them. Because the filling will be chilled, you may need to add another 10 minutes to the cooking time to make sure it's thoroughly heated through.

spring

spring

When spring gets sprung it's time for a big sigh of relief as everything comes back to life. After lying dormant for many cold, damp, dark months, new shoots start to appear from the ground and on the trees. At pieminister we love St Patrick's Day (17 March). As well as being Jon's birthday it's a good excuse to go to the pub, drink a pint or two of Guinness and try to dance like Michael Flatley.

Spring is also the time you'll need to start thinking about planting any veg you might plan on enjoying later in the year. We have our own allotment at PM HQ, and on pages 28–29 we've given you a few tips about what we've found works best planted where and when. Good luck and happy growing.

Vegetables
asparagus, new-season carrots,
new potatoes, purple sprouting
broccoli, radishes, sea kale, sorrel,
spring greens, watercress

Fruit
rhubarb

**Wild plants
(greens, flowers, fruit, fungi, nuts)**
alexanders, dandelions,
hairy bittercress, hogweed,
meadowsweet, nettles, watercress,
wild garlic, wild rocket, morels,
St George's mushrooms

Game
wood pigeon

Fish and shellfish
pollack, sea trout, wild salmon,
cockles, crayfish, cuttlefish,
langoustines

'the free ranger' chicken, cider & leek pie

Lying on the grass at the Orchard Pig cider orchards in Somerset, watching the blossoms blow down on a gentle spring breeze, brings a great feeling of wellness. A waft of this pie's big, deep, homely aromas gives the same feeling.

SERVES 8

Put the chicken in a large pot with the carrot, celery, ½ an onion, the garlic bulb, 2 of the tarragon sprigs and a little salt. Add enough water to almost cover the chicken. Cover the pan, bring to a simmer and cook very gently for about 45 minutes, until the chicken is cooked through. Leave until cool enough to handle, then remove the chicken from the pot. Strain the chicken stock into a clean pan (discard all the vegetables except the garlic) and boil until reduced by half – the flavour should become concentrated. Meanwhile, take the skin off the chicken and discard. Tear the meat into shreds.

Cut the rest of the onions into medium dice. Melt the butter in a pan, add the onions and cook until translucent. Add the leeks and cook until softened. Pour in the cider and simmer until reduced by about half. Stir in the flour, cook for a few seconds, then add 400ml of the hot chicken stock, plus the cream and the lemon zest. Bring to a simmer – the mixture should have a nice, creamy pouring consistency. Add a little more of the hot stock if necessary. Chop the remaining tarragon and add to the sauce, then remove from the heat. Squeeze in the flesh from the garlic bulb and stir in the chives and chicken. Season with salt and pepper and leave to cool.

Preheat the oven to 180°C/350°F/gas mark 4. Roll out the shortcrust pastry on a lightly floured surface to about 3mm thick and use to line a large ovenproof dish, such as a baking tin or lasagne dish. Fill with the chicken mixture and then brush the pastry edges with a little beaten egg. Roll out the rough puff pastry to about 3mm thick and use to cover the pie, trimming off the excess and pressing the edges together to seal. Brush with egg glaze and make a couple of small holes in the centre of the pie to let out steam. Leave to stand for 10 minutes, then bake for about 30 minutes, until golden brown. This pie is great served with roast potatoes and spring greens.

1 free-range chicken, about 1.5kg

1 carrot, peeled and cut into quarters

2 celery sticks, cut into quarters

2 onions, cut in half

1 whole bulb of garlic, top sliced off

6 sprigs of tarragon

a large knob of butter

3 chunky leeks, cut in half lengthwise, then sliced

200ml dry or medium cider, preferably Orchard Pig

2 tbsp plain flour

150ml single or whipping cream

grated zest of ½ lemon

3 tbsp chopped chives

1 quantity of shortcrust pastry (see page 10)

1 free-range egg, lightly beaten, to glaze

1 quantity of rough puff pastry (see page 10) or 375g puff pastry

sea salt and black pepper

'the chairman' beef, lager & shiitake pie

SERVES 4

'Preserve the old, but know the new,' says an ancient Chinese proverb. This is a beefy pie for the people, by the people. It suits simple and complex taste buds alike.

To make the filling, heat 2 tablespoons of the oil in a large frying pan, add the onion, celery and garlic and cook until lightly browned. Transfer to a large saucepan with a slotted spoon. Add the remaining oil to the pan, then add the beef and cook until browned all over. Transfer the beef to the saucepan too. Add all the remaining ingredients except the cornflour to the saucepan and bring to a simmer. Cover and cook gently for 1½–2 hours, until the beef is tender.

Mix the cornflour to a paste with a tablespoon of water, stir it into the filling mixture and cook for a few minutes longer to thicken slightly. Taste and adjust the seasoning with sugar and soy sauce if necessary; it should taste very slightly sweet, with aromatic undertones from the star anise and citrus. Remove from the heat and leave to cool.

Preheat the oven to 180°C/350°F/gas mark 4. Roll out the shortcrust pastry on a lightly floured surface to about 3mm thick and use to line a pie plate. Add the filling and then brush the edges of the pastry with a little beaten egg. Roll out the rough puff pastry to about 3mm thick and cover the pie with it, trimming off the excess and pressing the edges together well to seal. Brush the top with beaten egg and make a couple of holes in the centre to let out steam. Bake for 35–40 minutes, until golden brown. Good served with roasted sweet potatoes and wilted Asian greens, such as pak choi.

½ quantity of shortcrust pastry (see page 10)

1 free-range egg, lightly beaten, to glaze

1 quantity of rough puff pastry (see page 10), made with 1 tbsp roasted and coarsely ground coriander seeds added with the flour

For the filling

3 tbsp groundnut oil

1 red onion, diced

2 celery sticks, diced

2 garlic cloves, finely chopped

400g beef chuck or brisket, cut into 3cm dice

a knob of fresh ginger, cut into fine matchsticks

120g shiitake mushrooms, sliced

1 large cinnamon stick, broken in half

3 star anise

½ tsp fennel seeds

juice and grated zest of 1 mandarin or clementine

5 tbsp oyster sauce

3 tbsp soy sauce

40g yellow rock sugar (available from Chinese shops) or granulated sugar

600ml Asian lager, such as Tsingtao

1 tbsp cornflour

easter lamb pie

One of the great things about Easter is that you can get all your friends and family together, but without the build-up and pressures of Christmas. Most of the work for this sunny, zesty and classy pie can be done in advance . . . which means you can just chill and enjoy yourself.

Heat the oil in a pan, add the onion, celery and garlic and cook gently for 5–10 minutes, until just starting to colour. Raise the heat a little, add the meat and cook until sealed all over; don't let it colour too much. Add the wine and simmer until reduced by half. Stir in the flour, then gradually stir in the stock, herbs, lemon zest and anchovies and bring to a simmer. Cover and cook gently for 1–1½ hours, until the meat is very tender. Remove from the heat and stir in the artichokes, tomatoes and capers. Check the seasoning, then transfer the mixture to a pie dish and leave to cool.

Preheat the oven to 180°C/350°F/gas mark 4. Roll out the pastry on a lightly floured surface to about 3mm thick and use to cover the pie, trimming off the excess. Brush with beaten egg and make a couple of small holes in the centre to let out steam. Place in the oven and bake for 30–35 minutes, until golden brown. This pie goes well with minted new potatoes and fresh spring veg, washed down with a glass of chilled rosé.

SERVES 4~6

2 tbsp olive oil

1 onion, chopped

2 celery sticks, chopped

2 garlic cloves, finely chopped

600g shoulder of lamb, diced

1 glass of dry white wine

2 tbsp plain flour

600ml chicken or lamb stock

2 bay leaves

a small bunch of rosemary, leaves picked and chopped

a small bunch of thyme, leaves picked and chopped

grated zest of 1 lemon

4–6 anchovy fillets, to taste

200g jar of artichokes, drained and roughly chopped

150g cherry tomatoes, cut in half

2 tbsp baby capers

1 quantity of rough puff pastry (see page 10) or 500g puff pastry

1 free-range egg, lightly beaten, to glaze

sea salt and black pepper

baaa!

grow your own city garden veg patch

You don't need a lot of room to grow veg for your table, as most things can be raised in containers, and it doesn't need to take a lot of time. Regular watering is essential, but with a small plot a daily half-hour slot will be plenty. If your city gardening isn't going to end up as a fruitless task, then you will need a plan. Here are some essentials to get you started.

❶ Seed trays/plant pots/old yoghurt cartons

❷ Good-quality growing compost (preferably with some added natural fertiliser, such as well-rotted manure)

❸ Plastic cloches/old plastic bottles and/or a sunny, airy windowsill

❹ Vegetable seeds (choice depending on the size of your plot)

❺ A rough plot plan to keep your planting on track

❻ Gloves and a small trowel

❼ A pencil and ice-lolly sticks for labelling your plot

❽ A watering can

❾ A relatively good amount of sun

❿ Patience

Once you've decided what to grow draw a rough sketch of the area you have designated as your plot and plan in crops depending on their cultivation times (shown on seed packets). Opposite is a rough guide of when to sow crops that all suit a small space.

Most pests and diseases can be avoided with regular checking (pick off pesky caterpillars) and careful spacing (plants need air circulation to avoid moulds and mildews developing), so you shouldn't require the assistance of pesticides. If you do need to intervene try to use natural or organic products.

Companion planting is a good idea to help your chosen crops and divert or dissuade potential threats. Popular stalwarts include marigolds, geraniums, nasturtiums and sunflowers. Certain vegetables help their neighbours too, so be sure to do some research when planning your plot.

Be patient and savour every mouthful once you harvest!

Crop	Sow indoors*	Sow outdoors	Plant out	Harvest
Carrots	–	February to June	–	June to January
Leeks	February to March	March to April	May to July	November to March
Lettuces	January to March in coir pots or blocks	March to August	April to August (plant the pots straight in the ground)	April to October (you can also get winter-hardy salad varieties)
Peas	February	March to June	April to May	June to September
Potatoes	–	March to May	–	June to January
Shallots	–	February to March	–	July to December
Tomatoes	March to April	–	June	August to November

* Some plants, such as leeks, lettuces and peas, can be started off early by sowing them in pots indoors, and then the young plants are moved to outdoor beds or pots when it's warmer – or else you can sow direct later on. Others, such as potatoes and carrots, need to be planted where they'll be growing.

full english breakfast frying-pan pie

Forget Weetabix, this is the real breakfast of champions! It's super-easy to make, but you can also prepare the filling the night before, leave it in the fridge, then cover with pastry and bake in the morning.

Slit the sausage skins, peel them off, then shape the sausage meat into walnut-sized balls. Heat the oil in a saucepan, add the onion, celery and garlic and sweat for about 5 minutes, until softened. Add the bacon and cook until it just starts to colour, then add the chilli flakes, if using, the bay leaves and the sausage balls. Cook for about 5 minutes, until the sausage balls are sealed all over – try to keep their shape but it doesn't matter too much if they break up a little.

Stir in the tomato passata and the haricot beans with their liquid and bring to a gentle simmer. Add the black pudding and cook gently for 10 minutes. Season well, adding plenty of black pepper, then remove from the heat. Transfer to a metal-handled frying pan about 25cm in diameter and leave to cool.

Preheat the oven to 180°C/350°F/gas mark 4. Roll out the pastry on a lightly floured surface to about 3mm thick and use to cover the frying pan. Brush all over with beaten egg, decorate with the mushroom slices and sprinkle with the porridge oats. Make a couple of holes in the centre of the pastry to let out steam, then place in the oven and bake for 25–30 minutes, until golden brown. Serve with fried field mushrooms and fried eggs. If you're feeling really ambitious, and have some leftover cooked potato and cabbage, fry up some bubble and squeak too.

450g Cumberland sausages, about 6

2 tbsp olive oil

1 onion, chopped

2 celery sticks, chopped

1 garlic clove, finely chopped

180g bacon lardons

a pinch of dried chilli flakes (optional)

2 bay leaves

500ml tomato passata

400g can of haricot beans

200g black pudding, crumbled

1 quantity of rough puff pastry (see page 10) or 375g puff pastry

1 free-range egg, lightly beaten, to glaze

sea salt and black pepper

To decorate
a few thin slices of mushroom

1 tbsp porridge oats

spring chicken pot pie

Homely, wholesome and soulful food. Cooking the chicken on the bone gets even more flavour into the sauce.

SERVES 4~6

Heat the butter and half the olive oil in a large frying pan, add the carrots and onions and cook gently for 5 minutes, until softened. Add the garlic and fennel and cook for another 4–5 minutes, until just beginning to colour.

Meanwhile, heat the remaining olive oil in a separate frying pan, add the chicken portions and cook until browned all over. Add them to the vegetable mixture. Add the thyme and vermouth and simmer until the liquid has reduced by half. Stir in the flour, then gradually stir in the stock. Bring to a simmer and cook for about 20 minutes, until the sauce has thickened and the chicken is cooked all the way through. Stir in the cream and mustard, season with salt and pepper, then add the broccoli and parsley. Take out the chicken portions, pull the meat from the bones and return it to the sauce – or just leave the meat on the bone. We did! Transfer the mixture to a pie dish and leave to cool.

Preheat the oven to 180°C/350°F/gas mark 4. Roll out the pastry on a lightly floured surface to about 3mm thick and use to cover the pie, trimming off the excess. Brush with beaten egg and make a couple of small holes in the centre to let out steam. Place in the oven and bake for 30–35 minutes, until golden brown. Lovely served with new potatoes, tossed with spring onions and butter.

40g butter

4 tbsp olive oil

200g baby carrots, preferably Chantenay, cut lengthwise in half

200g baby onions, cut in half

2 garlic cloves, finely chopped

2 fennel bulbs, cut into 8 wedges each

2 poussins, cut into 8 portions each (or use 1 small free-range chicken)

a small bunch of thyme, leaves picked and chopped

1 glass of dry vermouth

2 tbsp plain flour

600ml chicken stock

200ml double cream

1 tbsp Dijon mustard

200g purple sprouting broccoli, trimmed and cut in half

a small bunch of flat-leaf parsley, chopped

1 quantity of rough puff pastry (see page 10) or 375g puff pastry

1 free-range egg, lightly beaten, to glaze

sea salt and black pepper

fat hen's hare pie

SERVES 8

Caroline Davey is a professional forager who runs wild food courses at Fat Hen in Cornwall. She showed us how many different foods you can snaffle up for free, including alexanders, which grow in the spring, and which we used in this dish. The hare needs to be cooked nice and slow for best results.

Put the marinade ingredients in a bowl, add the hare and marinate in the fridge for 4 hours or overnight.

Preheat the oven to 160°C/320°F/gas mark 3. Remove the meat from the marinade and pat dry on kitchen paper. Heat 4 tablespoons of the olive oil in a large frying pan, brown the hare well all over and transfer to a casserole. Remove the oil from the pan, pour in the marinade, including the vegetables, and bring to the boil. Add the beef stock and bring back to the boil. Pour this mixture over the hare, then cover the casserole and place in the oven. Cook for 3–4 hours, until the hare is very tender and starting to fall off the bone – keep an eye on the liquid level and top up with more stock if necessary. Take the casserole out of the oven, remove the hare and leave to cool slightly. Strain the stock and set aside.

Heat the butter and the remaining oil in a pan, add the baby onions, carrots and garlic (and the celery if you're not using alexanders) and cook gently for about 5 minutes, until golden. Add the bacon and cook for another 5 minutes. Stir in the flour, cook for a minute, then gradually stir in 750ml of the strained stock. Bring to the boil, stirring, until it thickens. Add the stalks of the alexanders and the sultanas and leave to simmer while you take the hare meat off the bone and shred it roughly. Add the meat to the sauce and bring back to a simmer. Remove from the heat, add the leaves from the alexanders and season with salt and pepper. Transfer the mixture to a large casserole or an ovenproof dish about 25–30cm square and leave to cool.

Preheat the oven to 180°C/350°F/gas mark 4. Roll out the pastry on a lightly floured surface to about 3mm thick and use to cover the pie, trimming off the excess. Brush with beaten egg and make a couple of small holes in the centre to let out steam. Place in the oven and bake for 30–35 minutes, until golden brown.

the legs and shoulders of 2 hares

6 tbsp olive oil

600ml beef stock

40g butter

200g baby onions, cut in half

200g carrots, peeled and roughly chopped

3 garlic cloves, roughly chopped

150g smoked bacon lardons

3 heaped tbsp plain flour

200g alexanders, stalks peeled and sliced, leaves reserved (if you can't get alexanders, use celery instead)

100g sultanas

1 quantity of rough puff pastry (see page 10) or 500g puff pastry

1 free-range egg, lightly beaten, to glaze

sea salt and black pepper

For the marinade
1 bottle of red wine

8–10 allspice berries

2 cinnamon sticks

8–10 juniper berries

6 cloves

¼ tsp grated nutmeg

2 carrots, roughly chopped

1 onion, roughly sliced

6 garlic cloves, bashed with the flat of a large knife

meat cuts

Here's our guide to the different cuts you can use for pie-making. It's a universal truth that the cheapest cuts make the best pies – you just need a little patience to give them the slow-cooking love they deserve.

lamb

❶ Neck Cheap and tasty, especially middle neck and scrag end. Both are melt-in-the-mouth when cooked slowly on the bone. Also good for turning into mince.

❷ Leg You can very, very slowly braise a whole leg after roasting it to make a lovely sauce and a good 'pulled lamb' pie. (But, to be honest, you can't do much better than roast it pink and eat it with mint sauce.)

❸ Shoulder Great when roasted or cooked slowly until it falls off the bone.

chicken

❶ Breast Good for a quick-cook chicken pie when used raw – but expensive and not as flavoursome as other cuts.

❷ Thigh Cheap and tasty when combined with breast for a mixture of textures. Best cooked on the bone.

pork

❶ Leg Best roasted, but also good for quick-cook pork stews for pie fillings.

❷ Belly Cheap, tender and fantastic flavour when slow-roasted.

❸ Hand Cheap and delicious: simmer until falling off the bone.

❹ Shoulder Great for pies when roasted. Buy cubed shoulder with a little marbling to get the best flavour. Also good for combining with pork belly to make a lovely mince.

beef

❶ Shin Cheap but wonderful when cooked slowly. Braise on or off the bone to get an incredibly flavoured sticky beef sauce. If cooked on the bone, allow to cool a little, then slip the meat off the bone.

❷ Shank Leg top, often sold as braising steak. Best cubed and used for stew; can be mixed with chuck.

❸ Cheeks Massively underrated, but fantastic when braised really slowly until they fall apart.

❹ Chuck Easily available but the most expensive of the stewing meats. Needs slow cooking.

❺ Hindquarter flank The belly – boneless, cheap and fatty but extremely tasty if braised very, very slowly.

❻ Oxtail A bit gourmet, but amazing in a pie. Cook for a minimum of 4 hours, let the sauce cool then simply slip the meat off the bone.

❼ Skirt Fab for pies, this cut is inexpensive, and very flavoursome for such lean meat.

❽ Brisket A cheap, boneless cut that if cooked long and slow will become very tender.

posh paddy's pie

Jon's birthday is on St Patrick's Day (17 March, if you want to send him a card). We decided to make this savoury cobbler for him instead of a cake, because he's sweet enough (apparently)!

Spread the flour out on a plate, season with a good pinch of salt and pepper and then toss the beef cubes in the flour. Set aside any remaining flour to use later.

Melt the butter and oil in a large, heavy-based saucepan over a medium heat. Brown the beef in it in batches – be careful not to overcrowd the pan or it will steam rather than fry. Remove the beef with a slotted spoon and set aside on a plate.

When all the beef has been browned, reduce the heat under the pan to low and add the onions and sugar. Cook gently in the butter and meat juices for 10 minutes. Add the garlic and cook for another 5 minutes, until the onions are a lovely golden colour. Stir in the tomato purée and cook for a minute longer, then stir in the carrots, celery, rosemary and thyme. Return the beef to the pan with any leftover flour. Add the stock, Guinness, Worcestershire sauce, mustard and green peppercorns, if using, stir well and bring to the boil. Reduce the heat to a gentle simmer, then cover and cook for 1½ hours, stirring occasionally, until the beef is tender. If it is still a little firm, simmer for an additional 30 minutes and check again. Adjust the seasoning and leave to cool.

Preheat the oven to 180°C/350°F/gas mark 4. Place the mixture in a large pie dish and lay the smoked oysters on top, then brush the edges of the dish with a little beaten egg. Roll out the pastry quite thickly on a lightly floured surface – it needs to be about 5–6mm thick. Cut it into rounds with a pastry cutter and lay the rounds on top of the filling, overlapping them like roof tiles. Press the pastry discs firmly to the edge of the dish to seal, then brush the top of the pie with beaten egg. Bake for about 30 minutes, until golden brown. This pie goes really well with a pint of Guinness and a dollop of steamy champ (see page 208).

30g plain flour

900g braising steak, cut into 4cm cubes

25g butter

1 tbsp olive oil

2 large onions, thickly sliced

1 tsp caster sugar

2 large garlic cloves, finely sliced

1 tsp tomato purée

2 large carrots, peeled and cut into large dice

3 celery sticks, cut into large dice

a small bunch of rosemary, leaves picked and chopped

a small bunch of thyme, leaves picked and chopped

300ml beef stock

500ml Guinness

a good splash of Worcestershire sauce

1 tbsp English mustard

1 tbsp green peppercorns (optional, but adds a nice bite to the pie)

1 tin of smoked oysters, drained

1 free-range egg, lightly beaten, to glaze

1 quantity of suet pastry (see page 11)

sea salt and black pepper

homity pie

A classic World War Two ration dish, adopted and made famous by veggie pioneers, Cranks. Ours has added 'hippity dippity doo dah' jazz hands! A big claim indeed, but one we're willing to stand by.

SERVES 4

First make the pastry. Sift the flour and salt into a bowl, add the butter and rub it in with your fingertips until the mixture looks like fine crumbs. Stir in the Parmesan, then add the egg yolk and about 120ml cold water – add about three-quarters of the water at first and mix to form a dough, adding the rest of the water if it seems dry. Knead lightly until smooth, then wrap the pastry in clingfilm and chill for at least 30 minutes.

Heat the oven to 200°C/400°F/gas mark 6. Prick the sweet potatoes with a fork and bake until tender. Meanwhile, melt the butter in a pan, add the red onions and garlic and cook gently until soft. Mix the Cheddar, spring onions and parsley together and set aside.

Cook the new potatoes in boiling salted water until tender, then drain very thoroughly. Transfer to a bowl and add the cooked red onions and the crème fraîche. Stir in the Cheddar mixture. Remove the sweet potatoes from the oven and leave until cool enough to handle. Peel off the skins and break up the flesh, adding it to the potato and onion mixture. Mix it in, trying not to let the chunks of sweet potato disintegrate too much. Season well. Mix together all the ingredients for the topping and set aside.

Reduce the oven temperature to 180°C/350°F/gas mark 4. Roll out the pastry on a lightly floured surface to about 3mm thick and use to line a 20–23cm loose-bottomed tart tin. Add the filling, then sprinkle the topping ingredients over the pie. Place in the oven and bake for 25–30 minutes, until golden brown. Serve with a herby salad (see page 209).

For the wholemeal pastry

350g wholemeal flour

½ tsp salt

175g butter, diced

2 tbsp freshly grated Parmesan cheese

1 egg yolk

For the filling

2 sweet potatoes

65g butter

1 large or 2 small red onions, sliced

2 garlic cloves, finely sliced

120g mature Cheddar cheese, grated

a small bunch of spring onions, sliced

a handful of curly parsley, finely chopped

550g new potatoes, scrubbed and cut into quarters

140ml crème fraîche

sea salt and black pepper

For the topping

a handful of fresh breadcrumbs

1 tbsp freshly grated Parmesan cheese

5 sprigs of thyme, leaves picked and chopped

pork, chorizo & prawn pies

Pure prawnography! In fact, so prawnographic that if this book didn't have a very strict sequence, this recipe would be on page 3.

Heat the oil in a pan, add the onion, celery and garlic and cook gently for 5–10 minutes, until softened and lightly coloured. Raise the heat a little, add the pork shoulder and cook for 5–8 minutes, until sealed all over. Stir in the chorizo and cook until it begins to release its oil. Add the fresh and dried herbs, the fennel seeds and the wine or sherry and simmer until the liquid has reduced by half. Stir in the saffron and paprika, followed by the passata, chicken stock and lemon zest, then bring back to a simmer and cook for about an hour, until the sauce has reduced and thickened and the pork is tender. Add the prawns and cook for 2–3 minutes. Finally, stir in the peas and cook for a couple of minutes longer. Season to taste and remove from the heat. Divide the mixture between 6 individual pie dishes and leave to cool.

Preheat the oven to 180°C/350°F/gas mark 4. Roll out the pastry on a lightly floured surface to about 3mm thick and cut out 6 pieces to cover the pie dishes. Brush the edges of the dishes with a little of the beaten egg and then cover with the pastry, pressing the edges down to seal. Use your imagination to decorate with langoustines or king prawns, if you have them – see the photos opposite for inspiration! Brush the pastry all over with beaten egg and make a small hole in the centre of each pie to let out the steam. Place in the oven and bake for 20–25 minutes, until golden brown.

2 tbsp olive oil

1 onion, chopped

2 celery sticks, chopped

2 garlic cloves, finely chopped

250g shoulder of pork, diced

150g cooking chorizo, sliced

2 bay leaves

a small bunch of thyme, leaves picked and chopped

a small bunch of rosemary, leaves picked and chopped

1 tsp dried oregano

1 tsp fennel seeds

1 glass of white wine or dry sherry

a pinch of saffron strands

1 heaped tbsp smoked paprika

300ml tomato passata

600ml chicken stock

grated zest of 1 lemon

200g peeled raw prawns

150g peas

1 quantity of soured cream pastry (see page 11)

1 free-range egg, lightly beaten, to glaze

sea salt and black pepper

6 langoustines, crayfish or king prawns in the shell (cooked or raw), to decorate (optional)

let's go foraging

While making this book we went on a fascinating foraging expedition in sunny Cornwall. Under the expert guidance of ecologist and cook Caroline Davey, of Fat Hen wild food school, we searched the seaside and the woods, and along fields and hedgerows. We found all sorts of tasty morsels and discovered that there is plenty of delicious free stuff all over the place — you just need to know where to look.

Here are our top 10 tips for foraging

❶ Start with species that are easy to identify. You'll soon recognize the strong aroma and leaves of wild garlic, and the signs of a hazel bush. Only pick what you have a 100% positive identification of – it's not worth taking chances as some plants and fungi are deadly.

❷ Take your foraging kit on walks or load it in the car when you go on trips:

- A basket – good for holding delicate leaves and mushrooms
- Several plastic tubs – many hands make light work of gathering fruit, and berries will get less squashed in smaller containers
- Scissors – use these to cut leaves cleanly
- Rubber gloves – for nettle protection
- Identification guides

❸ You don't need to travel miles to forage. If you have a garden, it may well have nettles, elderflowers in early summer and elderberries in autumn, and edible leaves such as bittercress and Jack-by-the-hedge.

❹ No garden? Then try local parks for the likes of crab apples, sweet chestnuts and walnuts.

❺ Follow the responsible foraging code. Only take very common plants such as nettles, alexanders and sorrel so that you won't be responsible for depleting stocks of rare species. Don't take the whole plant, but leave more than half of it to grow back.

❻ Do not trespass to forage for wild food. Either get the landowner's permission or stick to public footpaths. Only dig up plants if you have permission from the landowner, or if you are the landowner, of course!

❼ There are some precautions worth taking. Find out if fields have been sprayed before picking from them, and avoid picking along busy roads or immediately next to the path on dog-walking routes. Avoid riverside plants growing downstream of land used by grazing animals, because of the risk of liver fluke.

❽ Take only what you want to eat. Never strip the woodland or fields bare as other people might be hungry too.

❾ Start foraging at the seashore – it's the most productive habitat for wild food and many of the seaweed and coastal species are quite easy to identify.

❿ Organize your foraging expeditions with family and friends, bring back the wonderfully fresh seasonal produce and cook it together to create a feast fit for kings.

asparagus, pea & ricotta pie

This is a spring clean of a pie. Eat it with the sensational rice and herb salad and you'll feel the cobwebs disappear.

Trim the base off the asparagus spears and slice them into 1cm-thick pieces, leaving the tips about 4–5cm long. Put the asparagus pieces and half the tips in a large bowl. Add the ricotta, peas, spring onions, herbs, nutmeg, olive oil, lemon juice and zest, eggs and cream and mix together, seasoning well with salt and pepper. Transfer to a rectangular pie dish, about 30cm by 20cm.

Preheat the oven to 180°C/350°F/gas mark 4. Roll out the pastry on a lightly floured surface to about 3mm thick. Use to cover the pie, trimming off the excess, then brush with beaten egg. Push the reserved asparagus tips into the pastry so they stand up in a line down the centre. Place in the oven and bake for 30–35 minutes, until the pastry is golden brown.

Meanwhile, make the salad. Cook the rice according to the instructions on the packet and put it into a large bowl. Add the lemon juice and zest and the olive oil and stir gently to coat the rice. Pile in all the other ingredients and mix well. Season to taste and serve straight away, with the pie. It's best to eat the salad pretty soon after it's made, so the flavours and colours are really vibrant.

200g asparagus

500g ricotta cheese

200g peas

3 spring onions, sliced

a small bunch of mint, chopped

a small bunch of flat-leaf parsley, chopped

a pinch of freshly grated nutmeg

2 tbsp extra virgin olive oil

juice and grated zest of 1 lemon

2 free-range eggs

200ml double cream

1 quantity of rough puff pastry (see page 10) or 375g puff pastry

1 free-range egg, lightly beaten, to glaze

sea salt and black pepper

For the rice & herb salad

200g basmati rice

juice and zest of 2 lemons

4 tbsp extra virgin olive oil

100g flaked almonds, lightly toasted in a dry frying pan

20g mixed seeds

4 spring onions, finely sliced

1 large carrot, peeled and grated

1 fennel bulb, finely shredded

150g cherry tomatoes, cut in half

a bunch of mint and flat-leaf parsley, finely shredded

2 tsp sumac (optional)

i need a **pea!**

red pepper & butter bean 'bada boom'

A pie with a sunny disposition, delicious with a crunchy Greek salad.

Preheat the oven to 180°C/350°F/gas mark 4. Heat the olive oil in a pan, add the peppers and red onions and cook for about 5 minutes. Add the garlic and cook for another 4–5 minutes, until the vegetables are tender and lightly caramelized. Remove from the heat and transfer to a bowl. Stir in all the other filling ingredients and season to taste. Divide the mixture between 6 large ramekins or similar ovenproof dishes.

Mix together all the ingredients for the topping. Sprinkle the topping over the pies and then bake for 15–20 minutes, until golden and bubbling.

SERVES 6

4 tbsp olive oil

2 Ramiro peppers (the pointy ones), sliced into rings

2 red onions, cut into 8 wedges

3 garlic cloves, finely sliced

6 small tomatoes, cut in half

3 tbsp Greek yoghurt

400g can of butter beans or cannellini beans, drained

a small bunch of dill, chopped

a small bunch of mint, chopped

a small bunch of parsley, chopped

sea salt and black pepper

For the topping

½ ciabatta loaf, whizzed into crumbs in a food processor

a few sprigs each of rosemary, thyme and parsley, finely chopped

70g Parmesan cheese, freshly grated

3 tbsp olive oil

COME
HAVE!

I don't want
them you might
Toys for free!

how to throw a street party

The first street parties in the United Kingdom were the 'Peace Teas' held in 1919 to celebrate the signing of the Treaty of Versailles after the First World War. Since then they have marked big (usually royal) occasions as well as more local community events. In our hometown of Bristol the street party movement continues to go from strength to strength. Some streets here hold annual parties, with many 'competing' for the best entertainment, food, decorations and, of course, weather.

Community spirit reigns on street party days. Their recent renaissance has sparked other 'road closed' events, including the Playing Out movement, which encourages after-school road closures to allow children to 'play out' in the street without fear of traffic. A bit like in the olden days!

Street party tips to get you started

❶ Form a small street party committee and suggest regular meetings at least three months in advance to help to make your party a success.

❷ Apply to your local authority for a road closure at least three months before the proposed street party day. You will also need to write to local services (fire, ambulance and police) informing them of the application. Your local authority can usually supply template letters and give you advice.

❸ Write to everyone on the street inviting them to the party and informing them of the road closure application. You can download a template letter from the pieminister website or design your own. You might want to invite further ideas for the big day and let everyone know about the next meeting date in case they want to come along.

❹ You will need bunting – and plenty of it. Either get creative and make your own (get your neighbours to help) or ask for a small donation from each household to purchase some.

❺ Enter the pieminister street party competition – you could get free bunting, balloons and pies for your big day.

pear & chocolate pies

This little number is a quirky friend – you might not quite get it at first but once you do you'll love it forever. Soft pears, dark chocolate and rich pastry. Yum.

SERVES 4

Melt the butter in a frying pan over a medium heat and whisk in the sugar and cream. Bring to the boil, still whisking, and boil until you have a lovely toffee sauce. Take the pan off the heat and stir in the pears, plus any juice from the pears. Set aside to cool.

Heat the oven to 180°C/350°F/gas mark 4. Roll out the pastry on a lightly floured surface to about 3mm thick and use to line 4 individual pie tins, about 11cm in diameter. Spoon in the filling and top with a sprinkling of chocolate drops, then brush the pastry edges with a little beaten egg. Re-roll the pastry trimmings and cut out 4 lids. Use to cover the pies, trimming off the excess and pressing the edges together to seal. Brush all over with beaten egg and make a hole in the centre of each one to let out steam. Sprinkle with a light dusting of cocoa powder.

Place the pies on a baking tray and bake for about 25–30 minutes, until golden. Enjoy with lashings of cream!

40g unsalted butter

40g brown muscovado sugar

100ml double cream

6 ripe pears, preferably Comice, peeled, cored and thickly sliced

1 quantity of sweet pastry (see page 12)

45g dark chocolate drops, preferably 70 per cent cocoa solids

1 free-range egg, lightly beaten, to glaze

about 1 tsp cocoa powder

rhubarb & custard pie

Queen Victoria and Prince Albert, Noel Edmonds and Mr Blobby ... rhubarb and custard is yet another long and happy marriage that has stood the test of time. You may now kiss your pie!

Roll out the pastry a little thicker than usual, about 6mm thick, and use to line a 23cm springform baking tin, taking it up the sides. Be very careful that there are no cracks or gaps – if necessary, patch with extra pieces of pastry. Trim off any excess and chill for 30 minutes.

Preheat the oven to 160°C/320°F/gas mark 3. Line the pastry with baking parchment, fill with about 1kg of baking beans or rice and bake blind for about 30 minutes, until dry and lightly coloured. Remove from the oven, take out the paper and beans and leave to cool.

Arrange the rhubarb in a baking tin in a single layer. Using a vegetable peeler, peel the zest off the orange and add it to the rhubarb, then squeeze in the juice and scatter over the sugar. Cover with foil and bake at 160°C/320°F/gas mark 3 for about 15 minutes, until just tender. Remove from the oven, drain off the juices very thoroughly and reserve them.

Now make the custard. Slit the vanilla pod open lengthwise and scrape out the seeds. Put the seeds and pod into a pan, add the cream and milk and bring slowly just to the boil. Meanwhile, whisk the sugar and egg yolks together. Pour the hot cream mixture slowly on to the egg yolks, mixing constantly. Blend the cornflour to a paste with a very little water and stir in. Leave the custard to cool slightly.

Arrange about a third of the rhubarb in the pastry case. Pour in the custard and bake at 160°C/320°F/gas mark 3 for 20 minutes. Scatter half the remaining rhubarb over the top (adding it now prevents it sinking to the bottom). Continue to cook for 15–20 minutes, covering the pie with foil if the pastry browns too much. It is done when the custard is just set but still has a tiny wobble in the centre. Remove and leave to cool. Boil down the rhubarb cooking juices until syrupy and serve the pie decorated with the remaining rhubarb and orange zest strips, drizzling the juices over each portion. Serve on its own – three's a crowd!

1 quantity of sweet pastry (see page 12)

8 slim sticks of rhubarb, cut into 3cm lengths

1 orange

150g caster sugar

For the custard

1 vanilla pod

450ml whipping cream

150ml milk

65g caster sugar

12 egg yolks

1 tbsp cornflour

saint valentine's pie

This cherry and dark chocolate Bakewell heart is a long snog of a pie. Super-loving, it warms your heart just to smell it.

SERVES 6

Roll out the pastry on a lightly floured surface to about 5mm thick and use to line a heart-shaped cake tin, 18cm long, 15cm wide and 7.5cm deep (alternatively, you could use a 25cm loose-bottomed tart tin). Chill for 30 minutes.

Preheat the oven to 160°C/320°F/gas mark 3. Line the pastry with baking parchment, fill with baking beans or rice and bake blind for about 30 minutes, until dry and lightly coloured. Remove from the oven, take out the paper and beans and leave to cool.

For the frangipane filling, beat together the butter and icing sugar until light and fluffy, then beat in the eggs, one at a time. Mix in the ground almonds, flour and almond essence. Finally fold in the cherries and chopped chocolate.

Spread the cherry jam over the base of the pastry case, then add the frangipane filling. Sprinkle over the flaked almonds. Place on a low shelf of the oven and bake at 160°C/320°F/gas mark 3 for about 1 hour (or 40 minutes for a 25cm tart tin), until a thin knife inserted in the centre comes out clean; if the top colours too much during baking, cover loosely with foil. Remove from the oven and leave to cool for about 30 minutes, then carefully turn the pie out of the tin. Heat the apricot jam with a very little water and strain through a fine sieve. Brush all over the tart to glaze. Serve with a glass of Prosecco or a nice cup of Earl Grey tea.

1 quantity of sweet pastry (see page 12)

4 tbsp cherry jam

a small handful of flaked almonds

3 tbsp apricot jam, to glaze

For the frangipane
150g softened unsalted butter

150g icing sugar

3 free-range eggs

150g ground almonds

1 heaped tbsp plain flour

a few drops of almond essence

160g cherries, stoned and halved

100g dark chocolate (70 per cent cocoa solids), roughly chopped

summer

summer

Surfing, barbecues and picnics play a big part in our summer. If you plan your time well, you should be able to fit them all in over a sunny weekend. Luckily, based in Bristol, we are close enough to the west coast to get some great waves. If you are not from the south-west of England, then make a date in your diary and come to visit. Everyone's welcome.

Summer music festivals and weddings help make this the best season for partying. All accompanied, of course, by the great fresh produce you can get your teeth stuck into, from broad beans to strawberries.

Vegetables

aubergines, beetroot, broad beans, broccoli (calabrese), chard, courgettes, cucumber, fennel, French beans, garlic, globe artichokes, kale, kohlrabi, peas, radishes, runner beans, samphire, sorrel, spinach, tomatoes

Fruit

blackcurrants, blueberries, cherries, gooseberries, greengages, loganberries, plums, raspberries, redcurrants, strawberries, white currants

Wild plants
(greens, flowers, fruit, fungi, nuts)

horseradish, elderflowers, wild strawberries, ceps (porcini), chanterelles, field mushrooms, oyster mushrooms, giant puffballs

Game

grouse, rabbit, wood pigeon

Fish and shellfish

black bream, crab, crayfish, langoustines, mackerel, pollack, river trout, sea bass, sea trout, wild salmon, crab, lobster, scallops

jerk chicken pie

A strong contender for the 'you can put whatever you like in a pie' club. If you're ever wanting a killer barbecued jerk chicken, then look no further – this is the marinade for you.

Mix together all the ingredients for the marinade, add the chicken and stir to coat well. Leave to marinate for at least 2 hours, or preferably overnight.

Remove the chicken from the marinade. Heat the olive oil in a frying pan, add the chicken and fry until it starts to caramelize on all sides. Pour in the marinade and cook for about 5 minutes, until it begins to bubble and reduce. Stir in the kidney beans and coconut milk, bring to a simmer and cook for 5 minutes. Stir in the coriander leaves and season to taste, then remove from the heat and leave to cool.

Preheat the oven to 180°C/350°F/gas mark 4. Cut the pastry in half and roll out one piece on a lightly floured surface into a rectangle 3mm thick. Put it on a baking sheet and then put the filling on top, leaving a border all round. Brush the edges with a little beaten egg. Roll out the remaining piece of pastry and put on top of the pie, pressing the edges together well to seal. Brush all over with beaten egg and make a couple of small holes in the centre to let out steam. Place the pie in the oven and bake for about 30 minutes, until golden brown. Serve with a salsa (see page 210).

400g chicken meat, preferably from the thighs and with the skin on, diced

1 tbsp olive oil

400g can of kidney beans, drained

200ml coconut milk

2 quantities of rough puff pastry (see page 10) or 750g puff pastry

1 free-range egg, lightly beaten, to glaze

sea salt and black pepper

For the marinade

1 tsp fennel seeds

3 cloves

¼ tsp grated nutmeg

1 tsp ground cinnamon

2 tsp ground allspice

2 tbsp olive oil

1 red onion, sliced

4 spring onions, sliced

1 Scotch bonnet chilli, chopped, deseeded if you like

2 tbsp honey

juice and grated zest of 1 lime

juice and grated zest of 1 lemon

juice and grated zest of 1 clementine

a small bunch of thyme, leaves picked and chopped

a knob of fresh ginger, finely chopped

stalks from a small bunch of coriander, chopped (reserve the leaves)

'jamaica me love you' patties

2 tbsp olive oil

1 onion, finely chopped

2 garlic cloves, finely chopped

400g minced lamb

2 tbsp curry powder (mild or hot, according to taste)

1 tbsp tomato purée

150g peas

200g plain yoghurt

a small bunch of coriander, chopped

1 free-range egg, lightly beaten

sea salt and black pepper

a few fennel, cumin and sesame seeds, to decorate

For the almond & saffron pastry

juice of 1 lemon

a good pinch of saffron strands

300g plain flour

150g ground almonds

a pinch of salt

250g butter, diced

2 free-range eggs, lightly beaten, to glaze

Jamaican by name, Indian by flavour! These little babies will have you bumpin' and grindin' all over your kitchen. The quantities given are enough for 12 small patties or 6 large ones.

First make the pastry. Pour the lemon juice over the saffron and leave to steep. Put the flour, almonds and salt into a bowl, add the butter and rub in with your fingertips until the mixture resembles fine crumbs. Add the saffron mixture, followed by the eggs, and bring everything together into a dough. Wrap in clingfilm and chill for at least 30 minutes.

To make the filling, heat the oil in a pan, add the onion and garlic and cook gently for 5–10 minutes, until soft and lightly golden. Raise the heat, add the minced lamb and cook for 5–8 minutes, until browned. Stir in the curry powder and tomato purée, followed by the peas. Cook for 1–2 minutes, then remove from the heat and add the yoghurt and chopped coriander. Season with salt and pepper and leave to cool.

Heat the oven to 180°C/350°F/gas mark 4. Roll out the pastry on a lightly floured surface to about 3mm thick. Cut out 12 circles 15cm in diameter for small patties, or 6 larger circles about 25cm in diameter. Divide the filling between the pastry circles, putting it slightly to one side. Brush the edges of the pastry with a little beaten egg, then fold over to make semi-circles. Crimp the edges with a fork or your fingers, brush the patties all over with beaten egg and scatter with seeds. Make a couple of small holes in the top of each one to let out steam.

Place the patties on a baking sheet and bake until golden brown – 10–20 minutes, depending on size. Serve straight from the oven or leave to cool to room temperature. Excellent served with Encona hot chilli pepper sauce and a chilled Red Stripe.

the screaming desperado!

'Hola, chiquita! Una cerveza, por favor!'
**And make it snappy . . . This chilli con carne
is a dark, hot-headed Latino lover of a pie,
full of machismo. Good for the good times!**

Heat the oil in a large pan, add the vegetables and garlic
and cook until golden. Stir in the beef and cook briefly until
sealed all over. Stir in the cumin, oregano and paprika, then
add the thyme, passata, chilli paste and bay leaves. Pour in
the water, season and bring to a simmer. Cook gently for
about 2 hours, then stir in the cannellini beans. Continue
cooking for another 30 minutes, until the beef is tender and
the sauce has thickened. Remove from the heat, adjust the
seasoning and leave to cool.

Preheat the oven to 180°C/350°F/gas mark 4. Roll out the
pastry on a lightly floured surface to about 5mm thick.
Cut out a piece large enough to line a pie dish or other
ovenproof dish. Press the pastry into the dish, letting it
overlap the sides slightly, then spoon in the filling. Re-roll
the pastry trimmings to make a lid. Brush the edges of the
pastry lining the dish with a little of the beaten egg and top
with the pastry lid, trimming off the excess and pressing
the pastry edges together to seal. Brush with beaten egg and
make a hole in the centre. Place the pie in the oven and bake
for 30–35 minutes, until golden brown.

This tastes great with guacamole (for a quick home-made
version, mash up a couple of avocados with lemon juice,
Tabasco, crushed garlic, salt and pepper), and washed down
with a Sol or a Chilean Merlot.

2 tbsp olive oil

1 large onion, chopped

2 carrots, peeled and chopped

2 celery sticks, chopped

3 garlic cloves, finely chopped

600g beef skirt, brisket or decent
stewing steak, cut into 2.5cm cubes

2 tsp cumin seeds

2 tsp dried oregano

2 tsp sweet smoked paprika

a small bunch of thyme,
leaves picked and chopped

600ml tomato passata

1 tbsp chipotle chilli paste (or harissa)

2 bay leaves

600ml water

2 x 400g cans of cannellini beans,
drained

1 quantity of soured cream pastry
(see page 11), made with 1 tbsp
cumin seeds added with the flour

1 free-range egg, lightly beaten,
to glaze

sea salt and black pepper

pizza rustica pies

Admittedly we're stretching the definition of a pie here, but these are loved by kids and adults alike. They're fast cookin', great tastin', good lookin', so frankly, my dears, who gives a damn!

To make the tomato sauce, heat the oil in a pan, add the garlic and chilli and cook gently until the garlic is starting to colour slightly. Add the rosemary and cook for a few seconds longer, then add the passata, water and some salt and pepper. Bring to a simmer and cook for about 15 minutes, until the sauce has thickened. Remove from the heat and stir in the basil, then leave to cool.

Heat the oven to 180°C/350°F/gas mark 4. Cut the block of pastry into 12 rounds with a very small pastry cutter and then roll each one out individually into a circle about 3mm thick. Place on baking sheets and spread the tomato sauce on top. Scatter with the toppings of your choice, being careful not to overload them, then bake for 10–15 minutes.

SERVES 12

500g puff pastry

For the tomato sauce
2 tbsp olive oil

4 garlic cloves, finely sliced

a pinch of dried chilli flakes

a few sprigs of rosemary, leaves picked and chopped

300ml tomato passata

100ml water

a small bunch of basil, chopped

sea salt and black pepper

A selection of toppings
roasted aubergines

roasted peppers

sun-dried tomatoes

olives

cooked asparagus

rocket

freshly grated Parmesan cheese

well-drained buffalo mozzarella cheese, sliced

basil leaves

surfers' pies

The king of post-surf snacks, these are great eaten hot or cold. A similar pie, eaten after a surf at Bondi Beach in Australia, inspired Tris to say: 'Wouldn't it be great to have a pie shop called pieminister?' Lots more happened afterwards but it was another seed in the pot!

Heat the oil in a pan, add the onion and sweat for about 5 minutes, until softened. Add the chicken and cook until sealed all over. Add the sweet potato and cook for about 5 minutes, until lightly coloured. Stir in the curry paste and cook for a further couple of minutes. Add the coconut milk, bring to a simmer and cook until the sauce has reduced by half and the sweet potato is tender. Add the sweet chilli sauce, coriander and lime juice and zest, then season with the fish sauce. Remove from the heat and leave to cool.

Preheat the oven to 180°C/350°F/gas mark 4. Roll out the pastry on a lightly floured surface to 3mm thick and cut out 12 circles, 12cm in diameter. Brush the edges of 6 circles with beaten egg, put the filling in the centres and then cover with the remaining pastry circles, pressing the edges together to seal, or crimping them if you like. Brush with more beaten egg and make a small hole in the centre of each pie to let out steam. Bake for 15–20 minutes, until golden brown. Goes great guns with sweet chilli crème fraîche (see page 209).

SERVES 6

1 tbsp olive oil

1 red onion, chopped

200g chicken thigh meat, diced

1 sweet potato, peeled and diced

1 heaped tsp Thai green curry paste

200ml coconut milk

2 tbsp sweet chilli sauce

a small bunch of coriander, chopped

juice and grated zest of 1 lime

about 1 tsp Thai fish sauce
(nam pla)

1 quantity of rough puff pastry
(see page 10) or 500g puff pastry

1 free-range egg, lightly beaten,
to glaze

festival survival guide

We started selling pies at the Glastonbury festival back in 2004. Since then we've been to literally hundreds of festivals so we feel it's our duty to share some top tips for your weekend of music-fuelled mayhem. Ignore them at your peril!

10 essentials

❶ **Hat** Everyone needs a festival hat!

❷ **Wellies** Even if there is only a small chance of rain – and a plastic bag to put them in or sit on when it does rain.

❸ **Wet wipes** Showers are not nice places at festivals.

❹ **Painkillers** Do we really need to explain?

❺ **Head torch** Negotiating guy ropes and Portaloos in the dark can be challenging.

❻ **Glitter** You will be jealous of everyone else who has it.

❼ **Sun cream** You can but hope.

❽ **Sunglasses** Practical, you look cool and they hide a thousand sins.

❾ **Ear plugs** So you can sleep when you need to.

❿ **Pies** By far the best way to stay properly nourished.

10 luxuries

❶ **Teepee** Rent one on site and avoid all the hassle.

❷ **Box of wine/cider or crate of beer** On-site offerings can be expensive and difficult to transport so bring your own if possible.

❸ **Fancy dress outfit** Just because!

❹ **Air bed** Why settle for anything less?

❺ **Small bottles of water and Berocca fizzy vitamin tablets** The perfect way to rehydrate when you wake up.

❻ **A pack of biscuits** Handy in the morning before the traders open.

❼ **iPod speakers** To relax or get you in the mood.

❽ **Hip flask** Sneaky, but very welcome on a cold night.

❾ **Chair** Be the king of the campsite with a throne of your own.

❿ **Flag and a long pole** To help you identify your tent after a few ciders.

pieminister moo pie (well, almost)

Sorry, we can't give the exact pieminister recipe for this steak and ale favourite (it's a closely guarded secret), so this one's a slight variation.

SERVES 6

Melt the butter in a heavy-bottomed casserole on a medium heat. Add all the vegetables and herbs and cook for about 10 minutes, until beginning to colour.

Add the beef and cook until sealed all over. Stir in the flour, then add the ale, muscovado sugar, tomato purée and Worcestershire sauce. Mix together and season with salt and a few grinds of pepper. Bring to a simmer, put the lid on and cook over a low heat for 1½–2 hours. Remove the lid and cook for another 30 minutes; when done, the meat should be tender and delicious. Add lemon juice to taste (this just freshens the sauce a bit) and check the seasoning. Leave to cool, preferably overnight, so that all the lovely flavours can get to know one another.

Preheat the oven to 180°C/350°F/gas mark 4. Roll out the shortcrust pastry on a lightly floured surface to about 3mm thick. Line a large pie dish (or you can use individual pie dishes, as we did for the photo).

Roll out the rough puff pastry to about 3mm thick. Put the filling in the dish and brush the pastry edges with a little beaten egg. Lay the lid over the top of the pie, trimming off the excess and pressing the edges together well to seal. Brush the top all over with beaten egg, make a small hole in the pastry to let out steam and place in the oven. Bake for about 30 minutes, until golden brown.

50g butter

6 shallots, sliced

3 garlic cloves, crushed

2 carrots, peeled and cut into thick slices

1 bay leaf

1 sprig rosemary, leaves picked and chopped

2 sprigs thyme, leaves picked and chopped

600g beef skirt, brisket or a decent stewing steak, cut into 2.5cm dice

1 heaped tbsp plain flour

500ml real ale

1 tbsp dark muscovado sugar

1 tbsp tomato purée

1 tbsp Worcestershire sauce

lemon juice, to taste

½ quantity of shortcrust pastry (see page 10)

1 quantity of rough puff pastry (see page 10) or 375g puff pastry

1 free-range egg, lightly beaten, to glaze

sea salt and black pepper

pietanic!

The finest fish pie ever to sail the seven seas. A marvel, a wonder and a triumph to behold. Hopefully this pie will leave you with much happier memories than those of its namesake. Good luck and Godspeed, Cap'n!

Skin all of the fish fillets and place the skins in a saucepan. If the prawns come with their shells on, remove the shells and place in the same pan. Add the milk, along with the onion half, peeled garlic clove, bay leaf and peppercorns. Bring almost to boiling point, then remove from the heat and leave for about 20 minutes for the milk to be infused. Strain the milk through a sieve into a jug and put to one side.

Preheat the oven to 200°C/400°F/gas mark 6. Cut the raw fish into bite-sized chunks and combine with the prawns, half the grated cheese, the herbs and capers, if using. Season with salt and pepper and tip this mixture into a pie dish (or you can use individual pie dishes, as we've done in the photo).

Melt the butter in a saucepan and add the flour, stirring well to make a smooth paste. Cook gently for a couple of minutes, then gradually stir in the infused milk. Bring to a simmer, stirring all the time. Cook for a couple of minutes, then remove from the heat and season. Stir in the wholegrain mustard, if using. Pour the sauce over the fish. Gently mix all the ingredients, being careful not to break up the fish.

For the topping, cook the potatoes in boiling salted water until tender, then drain well. Mash thoroughly with the butter, a good splash of milk and some salt and pepper to taste.

Top the pie with the mashed potatoes, ensuring a nice even covering. Sprinkle with the remainder of the grated cheese and bake for 25 minutes, or until browned. Serve with buttered greens, such as peas, green beans or spinach.

300g smoked haddock fillet

300g fresh haddock or cod fillet

300g organic salmon fillet

400g cooked prawns

750ml milk

½ white onion

1 garlic clove, peeled

1 bay leaf

a few peppercorns

150g mature Cheddar cheese, grated

1 tsp chopped parsley

1 tsp chopped chives

2 tsp capers (optional)

60g butter

60g plain flour

2 tsp wholegrain mustard (optional)

sea salt and black pepper

For the topping

1.5kg floury potatoes, peeled and cut into chunks

50g butter

a good splash of milk

women and children dig in first

PLEASE
SUPPORT THOSE
WHO RISK THEIR
LIVES TO FEED
THE NATION
Royal National Mission To Deep Sea Fishermen

When washing up
Do not empty
any bits or grease
down sink as
it will block the
soakaway

Lift freezer
Door off very
carefully when taking
out ice cubes
as it has been
broken.

USE TANK WATER
ONLY FOR
WASHING UP.

'flying frying pan' smoked haddock & cider pie

Tris once spent what felt like hours sitting in the naughty chair facing a wall – he was four and had hit another child over the head with a frying pan (an early and promising sign for a chef). Thankfully, he has learned to curb such violent behaviour and now uses pans for more wholesome, culinary activities.

Cook the potatoes in boiling salted water until tender, then drain and leave until cool enough to handle. Cut into fairly thick slices and set aside. Preheat the oven to 180°C/350°F/ gas mark 4.

Melt the butter in a large, metal-handled frying pan (if you don't have one, use any frying pan and transfer the entire mixture to a shallow ovenproof dish before putting it in the oven). Add the shallots, leeks and garlic and cook gently until soft. Stir in the flour, cook for a minute, then gradually pour in the cider, stirring constantly. Bring to a simmer and cook gently for about 5 minutes. Stir in the mustard and cream and season to taste. Remove from the heat and add the fish, stirring gently to coat it in the sauce.

Put the sliced potatoes in a bowl, add the thyme or rosemary and drizzle with olive oil. Toss until the potatoes are evenly coated in the oil, then season with salt and pepper. Lay the potatoes over the fish mixture and scatter the Cheddar on top. Place in the oven and bake for about 30 minutes, until the topping is nicely browned. Goes really well with samphire that has been lightly steamed and tossed in butter, or with a herb salad (see page 209). And a big glass of fizzy cider.

SERVES 4

750g new potatoes, scrubbed

40g butter

3 shallots, sliced

2 fat leeks, sliced

3 plump garlic cloves, finely chopped

1 heaped tbsp plain flour

400ml good-quality medium cider

1 tbsp wholegrain mustard

150ml double cream

500g undyed smoked haddock, skinned and cut into large chunks

a few sprigs of thyme or rosemary, leaves picked and chopped

olive oil for drizzling

80g mature Cheddar cheese, grated

sea salt and black pepper

frisbeeeeeeee!

We have the Frisbie Pie Company of Connecticut to thank for the famous flying disc – or for its name at least. In 1871, William Russell Frisbie founded his family pie-making business in Bridgeport, CT, and local schoolchildren started playing with the baking tins, yelling 'Frisbie!' in warning as the pie plates came flying through the air. The sport was also picked up by Yale college students, who enjoyed a Frisbie pie or two on campus.

In fact, all kinds of lids, tins and plates had become popular for throwing games, especially during the Depression years of the 1930s. But the aerodynamic qualities of metal weren't ideal. In 1948, wartime pilot and small-time inventor Walter Frederick Morrison developed a plastic disc with business partner Warren Franscioni. At the time the skies were being scoured for UFOs, after witnesses in Roswell, New Mexico, said they had seen alien bodies at a crash site, and the disc was marketed as the 'Flyin' Saucer'.

Morrison later started selling a version he called the 'Pluto Platter', and that was when Richard Knerr and Arthur 'Spud' Melin came into the picture. The founders of Wham-O Toys, who had already spotted the potential of the Hula Hoop, approached Morrison on a downtown Los Angeles street corner in 1955 to offer him a deal.

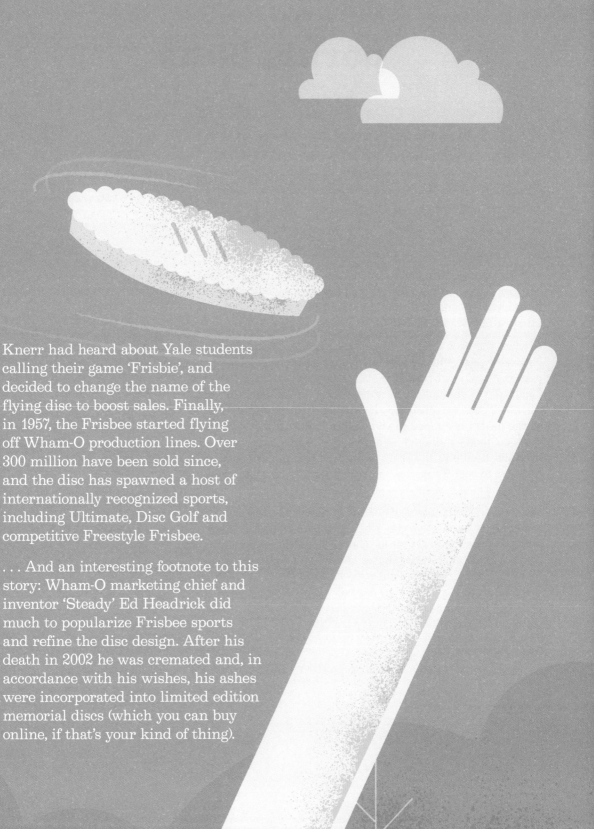

Knerr had heard about Yale students calling their game 'Frisbie', and decided to change the name of the flying disc to boost sales. Finally, in 1957, the Frisbee started flying off Wham-O production lines. Over 300 million have been sold since, and the disc has spawned a host of internationally recognized sports, including Ultimate, Disc Golf and competitive Freestyle Frisbee.

. . . And an interesting footnote to this story: Wham-O marketing chief and inventor 'Steady' Ed Headrick did much to popularize Frisbee sports and refine the disc design. After his death in 2002 he was cremated and, in accordance with his wishes, his ashes were incorporated into limited edition memorial discs (which you can buy online, if that's your kind of thing).

porkie buns

What could possibly be more satisfying than making your very own bun-shaped pork pies? Buy your favourite sausages, skin them and pop them into hot water crust pastry. It's as simple as that. Or you can add different flavourings – we've given a couple of ideas to get your creative juices bubbling.

Slit the sausage skins, take out the meat and put it in a bowl. Mix until it is fairly smooth. If you are making one of the flavoured versions, add the ingredients for the filling and mix well. Divide into 6 balls.

Preheat the oven to 180°C/350°F/gas mark 4. Divide the hot water pastry into 6 and shape into balls. Take a small pudding bowl – we used one about 10cm in diameter – turn it upside down and put a ball of pastry on top. Mould it around the bowl, then turn it the right way up and remove the bowl so the pastry is cupped in your hand. Place the pastry on a work surface – it should hold its shape. Add a ball of filling mixture, then pull the pastry around it and pinch the edges together to seal. Turn the bun the other way up, so the join is underneath, and place on a baking sheet.

Brush with the beaten egg and sprinkle with chopped rosemary if you are making the cheese, onion and chutney buns, or dried chilli flakes for the Vietnamese version. Make a small hole in the centre of each bun to let out steam. Place in the oven and bake for 35–40 minutes, until a skewer inserted in the centre comes out hot – a little liquid will probably be oozing out of the hole. Eat warm or cold. Great served with piccalilli salad (see page 210).

SERVES 6

12 good-quality sausages

1 quantity of hot water crust pastry (see page 11)

1 free-range egg, lightly beaten, to glaze

For the cheese, onion & chutney bun filling

100g Cheddar cheese, grated

1 small red onion, finely chopped

2 tbsp fruity chutney

a sprig of rosemary, leaves picked and chopped, to decorate

For the Vietnamese-style bun filling

1 lemongrass stalk, tough outer layers removed, finely chopped

a small bunch of coriander, finely chopped

grated zest of 1 lime

juice of ½ lime

1 tbsp sweet chilli sauce

40g roasted peanuts, chopped

Thai fish sauce (nam pla), to season

a few dried chilli flakes, to decorate

courgette &
chickpea filo pie

We get asked a lot to do vegan pies. This is
a yummy, must-have dish that goes down
a treat with meat-eaters too.

Heat the olive oil in a frying pan, add the onions and cook
for 3–4 minutes, until softened. Add the garlic and courgettes
and cook until the vegetables are just tender and lightly
coloured. Stir in the chilli, rosemary and thyme. Remove
from the heat and stir in the chickpeas, cherry tomatoes,
balsamic vinegar and extra virgin olive oil. Transfer the
mixture to an ovenproof dish.

Heat the oven to 160°C/320°F/gas mark 3. Lay out a sheet of
filo pastry on a work surface and brush with olive oil, then
scrunch it up loosely so it looks like a rose. Drop it on top of
the filling and repeat with the remaining filo to cover the
dish. Cover with foil and bake for 15 minutes or until the
filling is thoroughly heated through. Remove the foil and
bake for about 5 minutes longer, until the pastry is golden.
This pie tastes great with houmous.

SERVES 6

2 tbsp olive oil

2 red onions, cut into 8 wedges

3 garlic cloves, finely sliced

3 courgettes, sliced

a pinch of dried chilli flakes

a small bunch of rosemary,
leaves picked and chopped

a small bunch of thyme,
leaves picked and chopped

400g can of chickpeas, drained

200g cherry tomatoes, cut in half

3 tbsp balsamic vinegar

4 tbsp extra virgin olive oil

10 sheets of filo pastry

olive oil for brushing

isn't there chicken in chickpeas?

chilli 'pie-angles'

These fit beautifully into a lunch box, and are great for picnics and cheeky snacks. The roasted vegetable mix makes about double the quantity you need for the recipe, but that's all good because you can either: 1, make loads more 'pie-angles'; or 2, use the leftovers for a tasty and fantastic light lunch.

Preheat the oven to 200°C/400°F/gas mark 6. Put all the vegetables, chillies and garlic cloves in a large roasting dish, sprinkle over the cumin and coriander seeds and drizzle over the oil, followed by the chilli sauce. Season with salt and pepper, then place in the oven and roast for about 35 minutes, until the vegetables are tender and well coloured. Remove from the oven and set half of them aside for another meal. Chop the rest of the vegetables quite finely and transfer to a bowl with some of the cooking juices. Mix in the passata, tomato purée, coriander, oregano and paprika.

Reduce the oven to 180°C/350°F/gas mark 4. Roll out the pastry on a lightly floured surface into as thin a rectangle as possible – it should be about 1–2mm thick. Cut it into strips about 10cm wide and 30cm long. Place a little of the filling at the top of each strip, then fold one corner diagonally over it to make a triangle. Keep folding until you reach the end of the strip so you end up with little triangular pies, brushing the end of the pastry with beaten egg to help seal it.

Brush the pies all over with more beaten egg and sprinkle with a few chilli flakes. Place in the oven and bake for 15–20 minutes, until golden brown. Very good served with sweet chilli crème fraîche (see page 209).

SERVES 6~8

200g peeled and deseeded butternut squash, sliced

1 aubergine, cut in half

1 red pepper, cut in half

1 red onion, cut into quarters

2 courgettes

150g cherry tomatoes

2 red chillies

4 garlic cloves, left whole

1 tbsp cumin seeds

1 tbsp coriander seeds

2 tbsp olive oil

2–3 tbsp chilli sauce, to taste

100ml tomato passata

1 tbsp tomato purée

a small bunch of coriander, chopped (include the stalks)

1 tsp dried oregano

1 heaped tsp sweet smoked paprika

500g puff pastry

1 free-range egg, lightly beaten

sea salt and black pepper

a few dried chilli flakes, to decorate

mr & mrs hunt's wedding pies

Over the years, we've had the honour of looking after the food for some very special weddings. When Tris's sister, Imogen, and her fiancé, Sam, asked us to do a dish for their big day, we came up with these spinach, tomato and feta pies.

Preheat the oven to 180°C/350°F/gas mark 4. Put the spinach in a hot pan with a splash of olive oil, season with salt and pepper, then stir over the heat for a minute or two, until wilted. Turn into a colander and leave until cool enough to handle. Gently squeeze out excess liquid and roughly chop the spinach. Put in a large bowl, add the onions, cheeses, pine nuts, tomatoes and rosemary and mix well. Season to taste.

Roll out the shortcrust pastry on a lightly floured surface to about 3mm thick and use to line 4 small, deep pie tins, about 11cm in diameter. Divide the filling between them and brush the pastry edges with a little beaten egg. Roll out the rough puff pastry to about 3mm and use to cover the pies, trimming off the excess and pressing the edges together to seal. Brush with beaten egg and make a hole in the centre of each pie. To decorate, scatter with rosemary and put 2 tomato halves, cut side up, on top of each pie, pushing them down into the pastry slightly. Leave to stand for 10 minutes, then bake for about 30 minutes, until golden brown. Serve with mash (see page 208) and minted mushy peas (see page 209).

SERVES 4

200g spinach

2 tbsp extra virgin olive oil, plus a little for cooking the spinach

½ red onion, finely chopped

2 spring onions, finely sliced

250g ricotta cheese

200g feta cheese, cut into small dice

20g Parmesan cheese, freshly grated

50g pine nuts, lightly toasted in a dry frying pan

8 cherry tomatoes, cut in half

a small bunch of rosemary, leaves picked and chopped

1 quantity of shortcrust pastry (see page 10)

1 free-range egg, lightly beaten, to glaze

1 quantity of rough puff pastry (see page 10) or 375g puff pastry

sea salt and black pepper

To decorate

2 tsp finely chopped rosemary, mixed with a little olive oil

4 cherry tomatoes, cut in half

i love you, mash

i love you, pie

our favourite pie shops

Ye Olde Porke Pie Shoppe

In Melton Mowbray, Leicestershire, Dickinson & Morris have been making and selling pies at this establishment since 1851. A Melton Mowbray pie is distinguished by uncured, chopped meat and a bow-shaped outer crust. Melton Mowbray pies now hold 'Protected Designation of Origin' status and only a handful of local manufacturers are allowed to sell their pies as the genuine article. Beware cheap imitations!

Harry's Café de Wheels

Australian 'pie 'n' peas' phenomenon Harry 'Tiger' Edwards first served pies to sailors from a caravan parked at the Woolloomooloo dockyard in 1938. This Sydney institution, originally called Harry's, was renamed Harry's Café de Wheels after the city council ruled that mobile food caravans had to move a minimum of 12 inches a day. This café was the main inspiration for us when we first dreamed up pieminister.

YE OLDE PORK PIE SHOPPE

Harry's CAFE de WHEELS

pieminister

In this line-up, we couldn't not mention our original shop, which opened in Stokes Croft, Bristol, in 2004. Humble beginnings for the not-so-humble pie shop. It's still going strong and holds a very special place in the pie shop hall of fame (well, for us anyway!).

Manze's

Italian-born Michele Manze set up his first shop selling pie, mash and eels in 1902. By the 1930s there were 14 Manze shops across London. Most have since closed, but the ones in Deptford High Street (below) and Tower Bridge Road, Bermondsey, with their wooden benches and marble-topped tables, are still a big draw for Londoners.

smoked aubergine & olive strudel

If you like baba ganoush (smoky aubergine dip), then you will absolutely love this dish.

 SERVES 4

Prick a few small holes in the aubergine, put it over a gas burner and leave for 10–15 minutes, until blackened all over, turning regularly (you can also do this under the grill or you can roast the aubergine in the oven at 200°C/400°F/gas mark 6 for about 20 minutes until soft; it won't taste smoky, though). Meanwhile, heat the olive oil in a small pan, add the onion, green pepper, garlic and cumin seeds and cook gently for 8–10 minutes, until the vegetables are starting to turn golden. Stir in the ground allspice and cook for a minute or so longer. Remove from the heat and leave to cool.

Peel the blackened skin off the aubergine – it doesn't matter if there is a little left on. Roughly chop the flesh and stir it into the onion mixture. Add the tomatoes, honey, preserved lemons and green olives.

Heat a large saucepan, add a drizzle of oil, then add the spinach and some salt and pepper. Cook briefly over a medium heat until wilted, then transfer to a colander and gently press out excess liquid. Add the spinach to the aubergine mixture, together with the Greek yoghurt. Season with salt and pepper – you probably won't need much salt because of the preserved lemon and olives.

Preheat the oven to 180°C/350°F/gas mark 4. Place a sheet of filo pastry on a damp tea towel and brush with melted butter. Place another sheet of filo on top and brush with more butter. Repeat with the remaining filo and butter to make a stack of filo sheets.

Spread the aubergine filling along one short end of the pastry, taking it almost to the edges. Roll the pastry around the filling, using the tea towel to help you roll, and tucking in the pastry at the sides once or twice as you go. Turn it so the seam is underneath and brush all over with melted butter. Place on a buttered baking sheet and bake for 25–30 minutes, until golden. Remove from the oven and brush with a little more melted butter. Serve warm or cold. It's good with a herb salad (see page 209) and some Greek yoghurt drizzled with olive oil.

1 aubergine

2 tbsp olive oil, plus a little extra for cooking the spinach

1 red onion, cut into 8 wedges

1 green pepper, chopped

2 garlic cloves, finely chopped

1 tsp cumin seeds

1 tsp ground allspice

200g cherry tomatoes, cut in half

1 tbsp honey

2 small preserved lemons, flesh removed, skin chopped

100g green olives, chopped

200g spinach

1 heaped tbsp extra-thick Greek yoghurt

5 sheets of filo pastry

125g unsalted butter, melted

sea salt and black pepper

camilla's strawberry swirl

Come rain, come shine, Camilla (Jon's sister) has been the smiling face behind our Borough Market stall since 2004. Her feet must really ache! This recipe is dedicated to Camilla and her son, Dexter.

Preheat the oven to 180°C/350°F/gas mark 4. Roll out the pastry on a lightly floured surface to about 3mm thick and use to line a 25cm loose-bottomed tart tin. Prick the base lightly all over with a fork and leave in the fridge for 30 minutes. Line with baking parchment, fill with baking beans or rice and bake blind for about 15 minutes, until the pastry is dry. Remove the beans and paper and return to the oven for about 5 minutes, until lightly coloured. Remove from the oven and leave to cool.

Whisk the mascarpone and custard together until smooth and pour into the pastry case. Splash the strawberry liqueur or grenadine randomly on top, then take a knife and swirl it roughly through the filling. Arrange the strawberries on top.

If you want to decorate the pie with pastry hearts (see the photo opposite), roll out the pastry trimmings and cut out heart shapes with a tiny cutter or a knife. Place on a baking sheet and bake at 180°C/350°F/gas mark 4 for 6–8 minutes, until golden.

SERVES 8

½ quantity of sweet pastry (see page 12)

250g mascarpone cheese

600ml good-quality fresh custard

a few splashes of strawberry liqueur or grenadine

400g strawberries, hulled and cut in half

P.Y.O.

According to folklore, if you split a double strawberry in half and share it with a member of the opposite sex, you'll soon fall in love.

fig tarte tatin with pistachios

An aspirational tart, so to speak. This is the kind of pudding that you see beautiful people eating, from their beautiful table, in their beautiful house . . . Not that we're jealous or anything.

SERVES 8

500g puff pastry

16 small figs or 10 large ones

170g caster sugar

170ml water

30g unsalted butter

25g pistachio nuts, semi-smashed up, plus a few extra to decorate

1–2 tbsp honey

Roll the pastry out on a lightly floured surface to about 5mm thick and cut out a circle big enough to cover a 25cm ovenproof frying pan. Put the circle on a baking sheet, prick it all over with a fork and leave in the fridge while you make the filling.

Preheat the oven to 190°C/375°F/gas mark 5. Trim the stalks off the figs, then cut the figs lengthwise into halves; if using large ones, cut them into thirds. Put the sugar and water into the frying pan and heat gently, stirring to dissolve the sugar. Raise the heat, bring to the boil and cook without stirring until the sugar syrup has turned into a golden caramel. Reduce the heat and carefully add the figs – you will have to cram them in but beware, as the caramel will burn you if it splashes. Cook until the figs are tender but still holding their shape and the juices have run. Remove them with a slotted spoon and set aside. Boil the caramelized juices until thick and syrupy, then remove the pan from the heat and stir in the butter. Scatter the pistachio nuts over the pan and return the figs to it, cut-side down, in a neat pattern.

Put the frying pan back on the heat until bubbling. Put the pastry on top and tuck it firmly down the edges of the frying pan. Keep tucking it under to give a good rim and catch any escaping fig juices. Transfer the pan to the oven and cook for about 20 minutes, until the pastry is golden brown. Remove from the oven and wrap a cloth firmly around the handle. Leave to settle for a minute, then turn the tart out on to a plate. You might lose a couple of figs – just ease them out with a knife. If they don't come out at all, it might be overcooked – try putting the pan back on the hob for a minute to loosen the caramel, then turn out. Drizzle with the honey, and add a few more bashed pistachios, if you like. Serve with a bowl of Greek yoghurt drizzled with more honey.

tarrrt! how very rude.

autumn

autumn

There's some fantastic food around
at this time of year. Plenty of nuts and
fruits, and lots of lovely veg. Then there's
the game – pheasant, rabbit, venison
– which is increasingly considered a
wholesome, health-conscious alternative to
intensively bred meat. It comes from lean,
healthy, free-range animals and is low in
fat and cholesterol.

Autumn also brings a last chance to go
camping for the year and lots of reasons
to party . . . including Halloween and Guy
Fawkes night (or Pie Forks night, as we
like to call it). So get the fancy dress ready,
choose your fireworks wisely, start building
the bonfire and polish up your shotgun.

Vegetables

beetroot, borlotti beans, cardoons, celeriac, celery, chard, chillies, courgettes, fennel, kale, kohlrabi, leeks, peppers, pumpkins and squashes, salsify, spinach, sweetcorn, tomatoes

Fruit

apples, blackberries, blueberries, damsons, greengages, medlars, pears, plums, quinces, raspberries

Wild plants (greens, flowers, fruit, fungi, nuts)

nettles, watercress, bilberries, blackberries, crab apples, ceps (porcini), chanterelles, field mushrooms, oyster mushrooms, giant puffballs, chestnuts, hazelnuts, walnuts

Game

goose, grouse, mallard, partridge, pheasant, rabbit, venison, wood pigeon

Fish and shellfish

black bream, cod, mackerel, river trout, sea bass, sprats, squid, clams, crab, crayfish, lobster, mussels, oysters, prawns, scallops

glamping pies

SERVES 6

There is always some smug fellow camper who 'out-glamps' you. Nicer wellies! Bell tent! Bucket barbie! Blow-up bed! Plug-in car fridge! Don't get mad, get even. With this little number you'll outshine them every time. We've given you a quick-cook sausage and bean recipe, but you can use any filling you like.

First make your pie lids. This can be done at home up to 2 days before. Preheat the oven to 200°C/400°F/gas mark 6. Roll out the puff pastry on a lightly floured surface to about 5mm thick. Cut out 6 circles with a sharp knife, using an upside-down enamel cup as a template and re-rolling the pastry trimmings if necessary. Don't worry about the pastry being a little bigger than the inside of your cup as it will shrink when it is cooked.

Place the rounds on a baking tray and brush with beaten egg. Transfer to the oven and bake for about 10 minutes, until the rounds are golden brown and have risen. Allow to cool and then place in a Tupperware container or even one of your enamel cups, covered with clingfilm.

For the filling, which can be made either at home or at the campsite, first heat the oil in a pan. Slit the skins of the sausages and peel them off. Crumble the meat into the oil and fry gently until lightly browned. Add the onion and the garlic and cook until soft and translucent. Then add the tomatoes and drained beans and cook gently, covered, for about 15 minutes. Add the sage and cook for a further 5 minutes, until you have a thick sauce. Season to taste.

If you're preparing the filling at home, take it off the heat and allow it to cool – the remaining ingredients will need to be added when you re-heat the sauce at the campsite.

Once the filling is cooked (or re-heated), add the cream and Parmesan and stir well. To serve, spoon the mixture into the cups, place the pre-baked lids on top and present to your jealous fellow glampers.

6 enamel camping cups

150g puff pastry

1 free-range egg, lightly beaten, to glaze

2 tbsp olive oil

6 good-quality herby pork sausages

1 red onion, finely chopped

2 garlic cloves, finely chopped

400g can of plum tomatoes

400g can of cannellini beans, drained

a small bunch of sage, finely chopped

3 tbsp double cream or crème fraîche

3 tbsp freshly grated Parmesan cheese

sea salt and black pepper

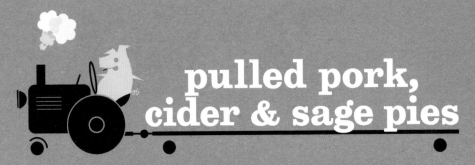

pulled pork, cider & sage pies

Perfect for those among us who own tractors and pigs. The pulled pork is so good we strongly advise preparing more than needed!

First cook the pulled pork. Preheat the oven to 180°C/350°F/ gas mark 4. Put the vegetables, garlic and thyme in a casserole, put the pork on top and season well. Pour over the cider and water and bring to a simmer, then cover and place in the oven. Cook for about 4 hours, until the pork is very tender, checking occasionally to make sure it is not becoming dry (add a little more water if necessary).

Take the pork out of the casserole and leave until cool enough to handle, then shred it by pulling it into pieces with your fingers – discard the fat. Remove the garlic from the vegetables, squeeze out the flesh from the bulb and set aside. Strain the pork cooking liquid and set that aside too – the vegetables can be discarded.

Heat the olive oil in a saucepan, add the fennel and onions and cook until golden. Stir in the flour and sage, then the garlic from cooking the pork. Add the cannellini beans and the liquid from the cans, pour in the reserved pork cooking liquid, season well and bring to a simmer. Cook for about 5 minutes, until the liquid has thickened and the vegetables are just tender. Add the pulled pork and season to taste. Ladle the mixture into 8 individual pie dishes and leave to cool.

Set the oven at 180°C/350°F/gas mark 4. Roll out the pastry on a lightly floured surface to about 5mm thick and cut out rounds slightly bigger than the pie dishes. Use to cover the pies, pressing the edges down on the outside of the dishes to seal. Brush with the beaten egg and make a small hole in the centre of each pie. Thinly slice the apple on a mandolin or with a sharp knife. Choose 8 good slices and brush them with a little olive oil. Cut a small star shape out of the centre of each slice to remove the core, if you like, then put a slice on top of each pie. Transfer the pies to the oven and bake for 25–30 minutes, until the pastry is golden brown. Great with scrumpy cider and baked potatoes.

2 tbsp olive oil, plus a little for brushing the apple slices

2 small fennel bulbs, chopped

2 red onions, chopped

2 heaped tbsp plain flour

a small bunch of sage, finely chopped

2 x 400g cans of cannellini beans

1 quantity of shortcrust pastry (see page 10)

1 free-range egg, lightly beaten, to glaze

1 dessert apple

sea salt and black pepper

For the pulled pork

1 red onion, cut into chunks

2 large carrots, cut into chunks

2 celery sticks, cut into chunks

1 whole bulb of garlic, top sliced off

a handful of thyme, leaves picked and chopped

1kg pork shoulder

375ml cider

600ml water

poussin boots pie

This chicken pie was inspired by that old feline charmer, Puss in Boots, who uses all his wiles and cunning to win the hand of a princess for his impoverished master. We like to use a normal-sized chicken, but feel free to try poussins. And don't forget to remove the boots before putting the birds into the pie!

You will need a saucepan large enough to hold the vegetables and the chicken quite snugly. Heat the oil in the pan, add the vegetables, bacon and garlic bulb and cook over a medium heat until they are turning golden. Add the mushrooms and thyme and then stir in the flour. Pour in the wine, place the chicken on top of the mixture and season well with salt and pepper. Bring to a simmer, cover and cook very gently for about 1 hour, until the chicken is cooked through.

Remove the chicken from the pan and leave until cool enough to handle. Strip off all the meat in largeish pieces and put in a large pie dish or ovenproof dish. Strain the cooking liquid and reserve, putting the vegetables with the chicken. Pour enough of the cooking liquid over the chicken to moisten generously (the rest can be served on the side). Stir in the prunes, then leave to cool.

Preheat the oven to 180°C/350°F/gas mark 4. Roll out the pastry on a lightly floured surface to about 3mm thick. Use to cover the pie, trimming off the excess, and then press down the edges to seal. Brush with the beaten egg and make a small hole in the centre, then scatter with a little cracked black pepper, if you like. Bake for 30–35 minutes, until the pastry is golden brown. This goes very well with Boursin mash (see page 208).

2 tbsp olive oil

4 large shallots, cut into chunks

2 large carrots, peeled and cut into chunks

2 celery sticks, cut into chunks

200g smoked streaky bacon, chopped

1 whole bulb of garlic, top sliced off

250g chestnut mushrooms, halved if large

a good handful of thyme sprigs, leaves picked and chopped

2 heaped tbsp plain flour

1 bottle of red wine (use a robust French red wine, such as Bordeaux)

1 free-range chicken, about 1.5kg

200g prunes, diced

½ quantity of soured cream pastry (see page 11)

1 free-range egg, lightly beaten, to glaze

sea salt and black pepper

make your own cider

Real cider is made from 100% apple juice with nothing added or taken away. Cider, or scrumpy, as we call it in the West Country, is a purist's drink and one we have been enjoying here for centuries. It is made by slowly fermenting the juice from crushed apples in barrels over the winter for a summer-long supply of refreshing apple heaven. You will find loads of advice online about making your own real cider and sourcing or improvising the kit, but here are some essentials to get you started.

Prepare your apples

Sort the fruit to remove any rotten apples, leaves, twigs and other orchard debris, then wash it.

Pulp the fruit

Mash the apples to a pulp, either mechanically using a scratter (a kind of apple-crushing mill), or by hand (pounding them in a tub with something heavy, like a chunk of timber). For small quantities you could use a tough domestic food processor.

Press the pulp

Use a cider press to extract the apple juice, which goes directly into a fermentation barrel. Wood was the traditional material, but these days the barrels are generally made from food-grade plastic.

Ferment the juice

Don't add yeast – wild yeasts occur naturally on the skin of the apple and are carried in the air. Cider fermentation traditionally takes place in an unheated environment, so the winter cold makes it a slow process. The cider is then left even longer to mature. Check your scrumpy in early summer for clarity, taste and specific gravity (you'll need a hydrometer for this, but it'll tell you useful things about the sugar and alcohol content).

Apples is apples is apples – right?

There are hundreds of varieties of apple but only a handful readily available in supermarkets. The best apples to use are those grown locally, so visit your local farmers' market or farm shop for advice. Alternatively, in the UK you can go to fruitshare.net to buy surplus orchard fruit, which would otherwise go to waste.

Most cider is made with a blend of apples – using both 'bittersweet' and 'bittersharp' cider apple varieties. It is also possible to use full-flavoured dessert apples, and add some crab apples for the 'bitter' quality. You will need to experiment to achieve your preferred blend but try to mix red, green and gold varieties.

You will need a lot of fruit: a gallon of cider takes about 36 apples.

A note about scrumpy

'Scrump' is a local West Country dialect term for a small or withered apple, hence the name 'scrumpy'.

love bunny pie

A 'tame' game pie for those just dipping their toes into the gamey waters of life. It's not without regret that we recommend young, plump bunnies as the best!

Heat the oil and butter in a large pan, add the rabbit and pancetta and fry until lightly browned. Remove with a slotted spoon and set aside. Add the vegetables to the pan and fry until lightly coloured. Stir in the flour, return the rabbit and pancetta to the pan and mix well. Pour in the cider and stock, add the porcini and their soaking liquid, then bring to a simmer. Cook gently, uncovered, for about 25 minutes, until the vegetables are just tender. Add the cream, mustard, tarragon and rosemary and season to taste. Spoon the mixture into a large pie dish and leave to cool.

Preheat the oven to 180°C/350°F/gas mark 4. Roll out the pastry on a lightly floured surface to about 3mm thick. Brush the edges of the pie dish with beaten egg and lay the pastry over the top, pressing the edges down to seal. Brush with beaten egg and make a small hole in the centre for the steam to escape. Bake for 35–40 minutes, until golden brown. Excellent served with mash (see page 208) and pea and carrot velouté (see page 209).

3 tbsp olive oil

25g butter

800g rabbit meat, diced

200g pancetta, diced

½ head of celeriac, peeled and diced

2 carrots, diced

4 shallots, diced

2 heaped tbsp plain flour

500ml dry cider

300ml chicken stock

25g dried porcini mushrooms, soaked in a little hot water for 10 minutes

200ml double cream

2 tbsp wholegrain mustard

a small bunch of tarragon, chopped

a small bunch of rosemary, leaves picked and chopped

1 quantity of rough puff pastry (see page 10) or 375g puff pastry

1 free-range egg, lightly beaten, to glaze

sea salt and black pepper

bunnies
love
pies

pheasant & bath chaps pie

SERVES 8~10

WARNING! This is not a middle-of the-road suburban pie – pheasant and pig cheeks equals foodie 'DynaMarmite'. This is a pie with plenty of front, attitude and bags of flavoursome fat.

First cook the Bath chaps. Put the vegetables, garlic bulb, bay leaves, wine and stock in a large pan and bring to a simmer. Add the pig's cheeks, then cover and cook very gently for about 3 hours, adding a little stock or water if the mixture becomes too dry. Remove the cheeks, leave until cool enough to handle and then roughly chop the meat. Be sure to include the fat – it will add flavour and texture to the pie. Strain the stock, discarding the vegetables, and set aside.

Preheat the oven to 200°C/400°F/gas mark 6. Season the pheasants, put them on a rack in a roasting tin and pour the strained stock into the tin. Cover with foil and place in the oven for about half an hour, until the birds are just cooked. Remove from the oven and leave until cool enough to handle.

Meanwhile, heat the butter in a pan, add the onions and bacon and cook gently for about 15 minutes, until they start to colour. Stir in the flour, then gradually stir in the stock from the roasting tin. Bring to a simmer and cook gently for 5 minutes.

Strip the meat off the pheasants and cut it into rough chunks. Add it to the sauce, together with the Bath chaps, and season to taste. Transfer to a large pie dish and leave to cool.

Turn the oven down to 180°C/350°F/gas mark 4. For the dumpling crust, put all the ingredients except the egg into a bowl with some salt and pepper and mix well. Gradually add enough water to bring the ingredients together into a firm but not sticky dough – you will probably need about 120–150ml water. Turn the dough out on to a lightly floured surface and roll out to fit the top of the dish. Push the dough down over the filling so it reaches the edges. Brush with beaten egg. There's no need to cut holes with this one – it's a flat dumpling topping, and you want it to steam a little.

Bake the pie for about 35 minutes, until the dumpling crust is risen and golden brown. Serve with roast garlic mash (see page 208) and braised red cabbage (see page 209).

a brace of pheasants

25g butter

3 onions, diced

200g bacon lardons

2 tbsp plain flour

sea salt and black pepper

For the Bath chaps

2 celery sticks, roughly chopped

3 carrots, roughly chopped

1 onion, cut into quarters

1 whole bulb of garlic, top sliced off

2 bay leaves

1 bottle of red wine

600ml chicken stock

800g pig's cheeks

For the dumpling crust

400g self-raising flour

200g beef suet

2 tbsp English mustard powder

1 free-range egg, lightly beaten, to glaze

Bath chaps are made from pig's cheeks; you will need to buy raw cheeks from a butcher for this pie.

wabbit rll

A wabbit, pork and black pudding roll, who would have thunk it! There are a few times in a cook's life when you think you've come up with something truly original. This is one of them.

Put all the ingredients for the filling in a bowl, add some salt and pepper and mix thoroughly. (If you want to check the seasoning at this stage, take a little of the mixture, shape into a patty, then fry and taste it.)

Preheat the oven to 180°C/350°F/gas mark 4. Lay the pancetta slices out on a board to make a rectangle. Spread the filling along one edge and then roll it up in the pancetta.

Roll out the pastry on a lightly floured surface to about 3mm thick. It needs to be slightly longer than your rabbit roll and about 3 times the width. Put the rabbit roll in the middle. Diagonally cut the pastry from the rabbit roll to each of the long edges in strips 2cm wide. Brush with beaten egg, then fold the strips over, alternating from one side to the other. Brush with more egg.

Place the roll on a baking sheet and bake for 30–35 minutes, until the pastry is golden brown and the filling is cooked through. You can check this by inserting a skewer into the thickest part – it should come out piping hot. Let the roll cool a little and then cut into slices 2cm wide. To serve, spoon some beetroot pickle (see page 210) over each piece.

SERVES 6~8

100g thinly sliced smoked pancetta

1 quantity of rough puff pastry (see page 10) or 375g puff pastry

1 free-range egg, lightly beaten, to glaze

For the filling

4 tbsp olive oil

300g rabbit meat, coarsely minced

200g sausage meat

300g morcilla (Spanish black pudding) or any soft black pudding, crumbled

60g breadcrumbs

1 tsp ground allspice

1 tsp mace

sea salt and black pepper

the world of pie

The World Pie Eating Championship is held annually in Wigan, Greater Manchester. The 2010 winner, Neil Collier, took just 23.91 seconds to gobble up a meat pie 12cm in diameter.

The first pie-in-the-face gag appeared in a slapstick comedy called *Mr Flip*, starring Ben Turpin, over 100 years ago. Since then, victims of a good 'pieing' have included Andy Warhol, George W. Bush and Bill Gates.

The world's largest pumpkin pie was cooked up in New Bremen, Ohio, in 2010. It weighed 1,677kg and was over 6m in diameter.

It is popularly thought that between 1644 and 1660 the eating of mince pies on Christmas Day was banned by Oliver Cromwell in England for being 'ungodly'.

In central Mexico you can eat *pastes*, which are remarkably similar to Cornish pasties. In fact, they were introduced to Mexico in the 1820s by Cornish tin miners who were employed for their mining expertise.

According to football legend, the chant 'Who ate all the pies?' was inspired by William 'Fatty' Foulke, who played in goal for Sheffield United and England during the 1890s. He weighed 24 stone.

In Russia, it was traditional for newlyweds to give guests a selection of pies on the third day after the wedding.

well, fact me sideways!

Samosas are among the most popular street foods across South Asia. Back in the 1300s they were a delicacy favoured by the Muslim aristocracy in Delhi.

King Ramses II, who ruled Ancient Egypt over 3,000 years ago, was apparently fond of a pie or two – there are drawings of bakers making pastry on the walls of his tomb.

Australians chomp their way through 260 million meat pies every year – which averages out at 12 per person.

sausage, cider & potato pie

Tristan first came across this pie at a Women's Institute fête. It's a real man's pie, he was told — but women will love it too!

SERVES 6

Cook the sliced potatoes in boiling salted water until tender, then drain and set aside. Melt the butter in a pan, add the onion and cook gently until softened. Stir in the apple and sugar and cook until the apple slices are tender but still hold their shape. They should just be starting to caramelize a little. Pour in the cider and simmer until almost completely evaporated. Stir in the mustard, season with a little black pepper and remove from the heat.

Slit the sausages open and peel off the skins. Mix the sausage meat with the potatoes, using your hands to break it up a little. Finally, stir in the warm onion and apple to give a loose mixture.

Heat the oven to 180°C/350°F/gas mark 4. Roll out half the pastry on a lightly floured surface to about 5mm thick. Use to line a pie tin and then fill with the sausage and apple mixture. Brush the edge of the pastry with beaten egg. If you like, you can add the Cheddar at this stage, pushing it down into the filling to make cheesy pockets. Roll out the rest of the pastry to about 3mm thick and use to cover the pie, trimming off the excess and pressing the edges together to seal. Brush the top of the pie with beaten egg and then make a couple of holes in the centre to let out steam. Scatter the herbs over the top, plus a little grated cheese, if you like. Place in the oven and bake for 40–45 minutes, until the pastry is golden brown and the filling is cooked through — check by inserting a skewer in the centre; it should come out hot. Serve with a WI-competition-winning chutney.

500g new potatoes, cut into slices 6–8mm thick

25g butter

1 onion, sliced

1 dessert apple, peeled, cored and cut into chunks

1 tsp sugar

100ml good-quality cider, preferably Orchard Pig

1 tbsp wholegrain mustard

500g good-quality herby sausages

1 quantity of suet pastry (see page 11)

a handful of grated Cheddar cheese (optional)

1 free-range egg, lightly beaten, to glaze

sea salt and black pepper

a little chopped thyme and/or sage, to decorate

steak & ox kidney steamed pudding

Deliciously old school! If pies (and puddings) were politicians, this would be a dusty old backbencher. Don't be put off, though — it's a damn fine pie.

SERVES 4

Heat half the oil in a large pan, add the vegetables and fry until golden. Heat the remaining oil in a frying pan, add the beef and kidney and fry until well browned — do this in batches, if necessary, so you don't overcrowd the pan. Add to the vegetables, stir in the flour and then gradually stir in the beer, followed by the stock. Add the bay, thyme, rosemary and some salt and pepper. Bring to a simmer, then cook gently for 2–2½ hours, until the beef and kidney are very tender and the sauce has reduced to a rich gravy. Remove from the heat, adjust the seasoning if necessary and leave to cool.

Grease a 900ml pudding basin with butter. On a lightly floured surface roll out the pastry to about 6mm thick and then use a large plate to cut out a circle about 24cm larger in diameter than the top of the pudding basin. Line the basin with the circle, making sure there are no holes in the pastry and letting it overhang the edges slightly. Add the filling, taking it to within about 1.5cm of the top of the basin.

Cut out a circle of pastry to make a lid, re-rolling the trimmings if necessary. Brush the edges with water and press it on to the top of the pudding. Turn up the overhanging pastry and press it down just inside the rim of the basin to give a really tight seal. Finally, run a knife round the outside of the basin to trim off any overlap.

Cover the pudding with a sheet of baking parchment, then a sheet of foil, and either tie with string or pleat the edges under the rim of the basin to seal. Either cook the pudding in a steamer over boiling water or place it on a folded cloth in a saucepan (a J-cloth will be fine), pouring in enough boiling water to come halfway up the sides of the basin. Cover and simmer for 1½ hours, checking the water level occasionally and topping up with more boiling water if necessary.

Remove the pudding from the water and leave to stand for about 5 minutes. Remove the paper from the top, run a knife around the edge and place a plate on top, upside down. Invert them both and lift off the bowl. Great with buttered carrots.

2 tbsp olive oil

1 small onion, roughly chopped

1 carrot, peeled and roughly chopped

1 celery stick, roughly chopped

300g beef skirt, brisket or a decent stewing steak, cut into 2.5cm cubes

200g ox kidney, white core snipped out, cut into 2.5cm cubes

1 heaped tbsp plain flour

250ml beer, preferably Butcombe

300ml beef stock

2 bay leaves

a small bunch of thyme, leaves picked and chopped

a small bunch of rosemary, leaves picked and chopped

a little butter for greasing

1 quantity of suet pastry (see page 11), made with 2 tbsp finely grated horseradish

sea salt and black pepper

fan-taffy pie

A robust veggie pie inspired by our Welsh friends just over the Severn Bridge. We need to tread 'Caerphilly' (sorry) but our favourite Caerphilly is Duckett's, made by our friend Tom Calver in Somerset (see page 182). Gorwydd Caerphilly is also outstanding.

SERVES 4

Cook the potatoes in boiling salted water until tender, then drain and set aside.

Heat the oil and butter in a pan, add the onion and celery and cook gently for about 5 minutes, until they start to turn translucent. Stir in the leeks and cook for another 5 minutes. Add the herbs, followed by the white wine, and simmer until the wine has reduced by about half its volume. Stir in the cream, bring back to a simmer and reduce that by half as well. Remove from the heat, season with salt and pepper and leave to cool slightly. Add the potatoes to the mixture, followed by the hazelnuts and cheese, reserving a few nuts and a small handful of cheese to decorate.

Preheat the oven to 180°C/350°F/gas mark 4. Roll out the pastry on a lightly floured surface to about 5mm thick. Put the filling in a pie dish, brush the rim of the dish with a little beaten egg, then lift up the pastry on the rolling pin and use to cover the pie. Trim off the excess pastry, leaving a little overhanging the sides, then tuck under to give a neat edge. Press down all round the edge to seal. Brush the pastry with beaten egg and make a hole in the centre. Scatter over the reserved hazelnuts and cheese. Bake for about 30 minutes, until the pastry is golden brown.

300g floury potatoes, peeled and diced

2 tbsp olive oil

25g butter

1 onion, chopped

2 celery sticks, chopped

2 leeks, white part only, chopped

a small bunch of thyme, leaves picked and chopped

a small bunch of rosemary, leaves picked and chopped

100ml white wine

300ml double cream

100g toasted hazelnuts, roughly chopped

150g Caerphilly cheese, crumbled

½ quantity of shortcrust pastry (see page 10)

1 free-range egg, lightly beaten, to glaze

sea salt and black pepper

ryan's cheese & potato pie

Jon first met Ryan at art college. Ever since pieminister began, Ryan has been responsible for our quirky graphics, which always make us chuckle. Despite a strange penchant for neckerchiefs, he's one cool dude. Thanks, Ryan, this one's for you! (For this pie you get a choice of toppings.)

Preheat the oven to 180°C/350°F/gas mark 4. Cook the potatoes in boiling salted water until tender. Meanwhile, cut the mushrooms into big pieces (field mushrooms into quarters, oysters and chestnuts into halves).

Melt the butter in a large frying pan, add the shallots and cook gently until softened. Add the mushrooms, followed by the garlic and fry over a medium heat until golden and sweet. Add the cream and simmer gently for a minute.

Toss in the parsley and season with salt and pepper. Add the sliced potatoes and the cheese, and give everything a good stir. Taste and adjust the seasoning if necessary. Spoon into a large shallow dish.

If you're using Topping 1, roll out the pastry on a lightly floured surface to about 3mm thick and lay it over the top of the pie. Trim the pastry to the edge of the dish and crimp firmly against it. Brush with the beaten egg. Make a small hole in the centre of the pie to let out the steam. Bake for 25–30 minutes, until the pastry is golden brown.

For Topping 2, mix the breadcrumbs and Parmesan together and sprinkle evenly on top of the pie. Place in the oven and bake for about 30 minutes, until golden brown. Serve with red cabbage slaw (see page 210).

SERVES 4

For the topping

Topping 1: 1 quantity of rough puff pastry (see page 10) or 500g puff pastry

1 free-range egg, lightly beaten, to glaze

Topping 2: 50g each of breadcrumbs and freshly grated Parmesan

For the filling

1.5kg floury potatoes, peeled and sliced

500g mixed mushrooms (field, oyster, chestnuts)

50g butter

5 shallots, thinly sliced

5 garlic cloves, finely chopped

100ml double cream

2 tbsp finely chopped parsley

200g fontina or Taleggio or Gruyère cheese, cut into lumps

sea salt and black pepper

booze matching

Want to know the perfect drink to go with your pie? Well, look no further . . .

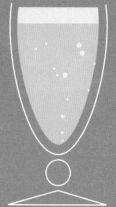

WHEAT BEER

butter 'nut nut' pie (page 154)

pietanic! (page 84)

homity pie (page 42)

LAGER

spring chicken pot pie (page 32)

ryan's cheese & potato pie (page 138)

the guru (page 146)

BITTER

'moo-dy blues' steak & stilton pie (page 172)

deerstalker pies (page 194)

pieminister moo pie (page 80)

SCRUMPY

porkie buns (page 92)

pulled pork, cider & sage pies (page 116)

pork, chorizo & prawn pies (page 44)

XXX

DRY CIDER

the free ranger (page 22)

christingle pies (page 190)

pizza rustica pies (page 74)

SWEET CIDER

surfers' pies (page 76)

red pepper & butter bean bada boom (page 50)

rhubarb & custard pie (page 58)

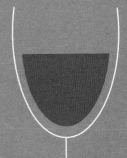

thali café paneer, spinach & pea pies

The Thali Café is another Bristol institution that started out at festivals. This dish stars paneer, a cheese that is found throughout India and makes a good alternative to meat.

Heat the 70ml of vegetable oil in a heavy-based frying pan until spitting hot. Add the diced paneer and fry until golden brown. Remove from the pan and keep to one side.

Now make the sauce. Heat the 50ml of oil in a clean frying pan, add the onion, cumin seeds, ginger, garlic and chillies and fry until the onion is translucent. Add the ground cumin, coriander and turmeric and stir until the onion mixture is coated in the spices and gently sizzling. Add the fresh and canned tomatoes, spinach and peas and cook briefly until the spinach has wilted. Stir in the fried paneer and cream, then add the methi and cardamom. Season to taste with salt, remove from the heat and leave to cool.

Preheat the oven to 180°C/350°F/gas mark 4. Roll out half the pastry on a lightly floured surface to about 5mm thick and use to line 4 individual pie dishes. Spoon in the filling and brush the pastry edges with a little beaten egg. Roll out the rest of the pastry and cut it to fit the tops of the pies. Cover the pies with the pastry and press the edges down well to seal, then brush with beaten egg. Make a hole in the middle of each one to let out the steam. Place in the oven and bake for about 30 minutes, until the pastry is browned. Serve with a selection of Indian chutneys and pickles.

SERVES 4

70ml vegetable oil

350g paneer cheese, diced

1 quantity of shortcrust pastry (see page 10)

1 free-range egg, lightly beaten

For the sauce

50ml vegetable oil

1 onion, sliced

1 heaped tsp cumin seeds

a thumb-sized piece of fresh ginger, finely chopped

5 garlic cloves, finely chopped

2–3 green chillies, finely chopped

1 heaped tsp ground cumin

1 heaped tsp ground coriander

1 tsp ground turmeric

4 large tomatoes, roughly chopped

half a 400g can of chopped tomatoes

500g spinach, roughly chopped

150g peas

200ml double cream

1 tsp ground methi (fenugreek)

½ tsp ground cardamom

sea salt

chicken &
butternut squash
curry pie

The filling for this pie is based on an old family recipe from Thali Café chef, Prasad. Cooking the chicken thighs on the bone gives a better flavour.

Mix together all the ingredients for the spice mix and rub them on to the chicken thighs. Leave in the fridge for at least 2 hours so the spices really flavour the meat. Meanwhile, cook the butternut squash in boiling salted water until just tender to the point of a knife, then drain and set aside.

Heat the oil in a heavy frying pan or wok. When spitting hot, carefully add the chicken thighs and fry until just browned (the chicken doesn't need to be fully cooked at this point). Remove the chicken and keep to one side. Add the onions, garlic, ginger and green pepper to the pan and fry gently until the onions are translucent. Then add the cinnamon, cardamom and star anise and stir until the whole mixture is sizzling. Add the chillies, fresh and canned tomatoes and tomato purée, bring to simmering point, then return the chicken thighs to the pan. Turn down the heat and cook for about 15 minutes, stirring occasionally, until the chicken is cooked through and tender. Season with the salt, then turn off the heat and leave the mixture to cool a little.

Next, the messy bit. Pull the meat from the bones and remove the cinnamon stick, cardamom pods and star anise from the mixture. Return the thigh meat to the sauce, along with the butternut squash. Stir to coat thoroughly, then leave to cool.

Preheat the oven to 180°C/350°F/gas mark 4. Roll out half the pastry on a lightly floured surface to about 5mm thick and use to line a pie dish. Fill with the chicken curry. Brush the pastry edges with beaten egg.

Roll out the remaining pastry and use to cover the pie, pressing the pastry edges together to seal and trimming off the excess. Brush all over with beaten egg and make a hole in the centre to let out the steam. Scatter over the fennel seeds and dried chilli flakes and decorate with the star anise. Bake for about 30 minutes, until the pastry is golden brown.

800g free-range chicken thighs

500g butternut squash, peeled, deseeded and cut into 3cm cubes

70ml vegetable oil

4 onions, roughly chopped

8 garlic cloves, finely chopped

a thumb-sized piece of fresh ginger, finely chopped

1 green pepper, roughly diced

1 large cinnamon stick, broken up

6 green cardamom pods

8 star anise

6–8 green chillies, chopped

8 large tomatoes, roughly chopped

400g can of chopped tomatoes

2 tbsp tomato purée

2 tsp salt, or to taste

1 quantity of shortcrust pastry (see page 10)

1 free-range egg, lightly beaten

1 tsp fennel seeds

1 tsp dried chilli flakes

1 star anise

For the spice mix

2 tsp chilli powder

a thumb-sized piece of fresh ginger, finely chopped

1 tsp ground turmeric

1 tsp paprika

a few grinds of black pepper

the guru

Curry reminds Tris of his dad, who made a killer curry and absolutely loved India. He knew one Hindi sentence: 'I have just shot a tiger and wonder if you would be so kind as to help me take it home.' Once, he recited this when we were out and the waiter promptly replied, 'Would you like a naan bread with that, sir?' For this lamb dansak pie you won't need the quantity given below — serve about two-thirds of it as a curry, then use the leftovers the next day to make a pie.

Heat the oil in a large pan. When it is quite hot, add the lamb and cook until browned all over. Add the onions, ginger and chillies, reduce the heat and cook until the onions are soft. Add the cinnamon stick, turmeric, coriander and chilli powder and cook, stirring, for about a minute — work quickly so they don't burn. Next add the yellow and red lentils, stir well, then add the chickpeas and their liquid, plus the cardamom, cloves and curry leaves. Pour in the passata and water, bring to the boil and simmer very gently for 1¼ hours.

Add the pumpkin, squash or sweet potato and cook for 30 minutes, then stir in the spinach, chopped tomatoes and coriander. Cook for another 10 minutes, squeeze in the lime juice and season to taste, adding more lime or chilli if you like — it should be aromatic, tart and spicy. Leave to cool.

Preheat the oven to 180°C/350°F/gas mark 4. Roll out about two-thirds of the pastry on a lightly floured surface to about 3mm thick and use to line a 28cm loose-bottomed tart tin. Add the filling, then roll out the remaining pastry to make a lid. Brush the edges of the pastry in the tin with a little beaten egg, cover with the pastry lid and trim off the excess, pressing the edges together to seal. Brush all over with beaten egg and make a small hole in the centre. You could scatter the top with coriander seeds or chopped fresh chilli, if you like. Bake for 30–35 minutes, until the pastry is golden brown. Serve with a salsa (see page 210).

4 tbsp vegetable oil

600g lamb neck fillet, cut into cubes

2 onions, sliced

8cm piece of fresh ginger, peeled and finely grated

3 green chillies, finely chopped

1 cinnamon stick

1 tsp ground turmeric

2 tbsp ground coriander

1 tsp chilli powder (preferably Kashmiri)

120g yellow lentils

120g red lentils

400g can of chickpeas

4 cardamom pods

3 cloves

a small handful of curry leaves

500ml tomato passata

1 litre water

200g pumpkin, squash or sweet potato, peeled and cut into cubes

300g fresh spinach, shredded

3 tomatoes, chopped

a bunch of coriander, chopped

juice of 2 limes

1 quantity of shortcrust pastry (see page 10), made with wholemeal flour and 1 rounded tbsp nigella (black onion) seeds

1 free-range egg, lightly beaten

sea salt and black pepper

I LIKE TO BE
TURNED ON
AT ALL TIMES!

the life* and pies of sweeney todd

The story goes that Sweeney Todd, the Demon Barber of Fleet Street, was born in Brick Lane in 1756. At the age of 14 the young Todd was sentenced to five years in Newgate Prison, after being wrongly accused of stealing a watch. There, he was soon befriended by a dodgy barber called Elmer Plummer, who taught Sweeney how to pickpocket other inmates while giving them a shave.

Soon after leaving prison, and having saved a few pounds, Sweeney set up a small barber's shop at 186 Fleet Street. But this was no ordinary shop – it was fitted with a barber's chair sat on a revolving trapdoor. Unsuspecting customers would settle in for their shave or haircut, only to be flipped over and dropped on their heads into the cellar below. While they lay unconscious, the barber would run down the stairs and slit their throats with his razor.

Sweeney's lover Margery Lovett had a pie shop in nearby Bell Yard, and the pair discovered a tunnel between his cellar and her pie shop. This gave them the perfect opportunity to dispose of the corpses: Mrs Lovett's pies were filled with human flesh.

Her shop was one of the most celebrated in London. The fame of its veal and pork pies spread far and wide, and at 12 o'clock every day, when the pies came out of the oven, huge queues formed.

By the time of Sweeney's capture in 1802 he had killed more than 150 people, making him the most prolific murderer in London's history. He was hanged in front of thousands of onlookers. Mrs Lovett was sent to Newgate Prison, but shortly after was found poisoned in her cell.

* In fact, it is hotly disputed whether Sweeney Todd ever lived at all. Many believe he was 'born' in *The String of Pearls*, a story in a 'penny dreadful' magazine of 1846. Our account is based on the work of historian Peter Haining, who claims to have discovered the evidence for Todd's real existence after 25 years of research.

romany's lucky ducky pies

Romany's pie revelation! Being Tris's sister, Jon's wife, mum of two pie-'mini'-sters and our formidable press officer, she doesn't have time to pluck a duck, so came up with this absolute 'quacker' of a cheat. It uses confit duck legs, which you can find in delis and some supermarkets. This is probably the best recipe in the book! Thanks, Pom Pom! xxx

Melt the butter in a pan, add the shallots and cook gently for 4–5 minutes, until lightly coloured. Stir in the garlic and red cabbage, then add the vinegar, cider, sugar, star anise and cinnamon. Bring to a simmer and cook over a medium heat for 20–25 minutes, until the butter and sugar start to caramelize the cabbage and the liquid reduces to a glaze. Season with salt and pepper, add the pears and cook for about 5 minutes, until they are just tender but still holding their shape.

Remove the skin from the confit duck legs – but don't throw it away! If you put it in the oven to crisp up while the pie is baking, it makes a delicious nibble. Shred the duck meat into the cabbage and then transfer the mixture to 4 individual pie dishes. Preheat the oven to 180°C/350°F/gas mark 4.

For the topping, cook the potatoes in boiling salted water until tender, then drain well. Mash with the butter and cream and season to taste. Top the pies with the mash, place in the oven and bake for 20–25 minutes, until golden. Delicious served with pea and carrot velouté (see page 209).

SERVES 4

50g butter

3 shallots, sliced

2 garlic cloves, chopped

¼ small red cabbage, about 150g, shredded

2 tbsp cider vinegar

150ml dry cider

2 tbsp demerara sugar

2 star anise

½ tsp ground cinnamon

2 Williams pears, peeled, cored and roughly chopped

2 confit duck legs, shredded

sea salt and black pepper

For the topping

500g floury potatoes, peeled and cut into chunks

50g butter

100ml double cream

butter 'nut nut' pie

If squirrels ate pies, they'd eat this one. Riffing on the classic American pumpkin pie, we've used butternut squash instead. It works brilliantly and, frankly, is a lot less hassle to deal with. The maple nut topping is a triumph.

SERVES 6

Preheat the oven to 180°C/350°F/gas mark 4. Roll out the pastry on a lightly floured surface to about 3mm thick and use to line a 25cm loose-bottomed tart tin, trimming off the excess. Cover with baking parchment, fill with baking beans or rice and bake blind for 15–20 minutes, until the pastry is cooked and lightly coloured. Remove from the oven, take out the paper and beans or rice and leave to cool.

Cook the butternut squash in a large pan of boiling water until tender to the point of a knife. Drain thoroughly. Transfer to a blender or food processor, add the cream, eggs, sugar and nutmeg and blitz until smooth. Leave to cool.

For the topping, pulse the nuts in a food processor until roughly crumbled. Tip into a bowl and stir in the pumpkin seeds and maple syrup. Set aside.

Pour the butternut purée into the pastry case and bake at 180°C/350°F/gas mark 4 for about 20 minutes, until the filling is just firm to the touch. Sprinkle over the nuts and return the pie to the oven for about 10 minutes, until the topping is golden brown. Drizzle with extra maple syrup. Serve warm with ice cream (see page 211), or at room temperature.

½ quantity of shortcrust pastry (see page 10)

500g butternut squash (peeled weight), diced

200ml double cream

2 free-range eggs

80g light soft brown sugar

1 tsp grated nutmeg

For the topping
100g blanched almonds

100g skinned hazelnuts

100g pecan nuts

40g pumpkin seeds

4 tbsp maple syrup, plus extra for drizzling

this is one big nut

blackberry & apple pie

Everyone thinks they make the best blackberry and apple pie. Well, they don't . . . Ange in our kitchens does. Luckily for you, she's one of life's givers! Ange, God bless you and your pud.

Melt half the butter in a shallow pan over a medium heat. When the butter is hot and bubbling, add half the Bramley and Cox's apples and cook until golden and almost tender, turning once to cook the other side. Add half the spiced sugar and cook until the mixture starts to caramelize. Pour the apples into a dish and cook the remaining apples in the same way with the rest of the butter and spiced sugar. When complete, put the apples to one side and leave to cool. (The reason we don't do all the apples at once is because it's very difficult to get good, even caramelization if you overcrowd the pan.)

Preheat the oven to 180°C/350°F/gas 4. Roll out half the pastry on a lightly floured surface to about 5mm thick. Line a shallow 26cm pie dish with the pastry, trimming off any excess around the edges using a sharp knife. Tip the cooled apples into the lined pie dish, and sprinkle with the blackberries.

Brush the edge of the pastry with beaten egg. Roll out the other half of the pastry and lay it over the top of the pie. Trim the edges and crimp them together with your fingers. Brush the top of the pie with beaten egg, sprinkle generously with the cinnamon sugar and make a couple of slashes in the top of the pastry.

Place the pie on a baking tray and then put it directly on the bottom of the oven. Cook for 55–60 minutes, until the pastry is golden brown and crisp. Serve with clotted cream, ice cream or custard (see page 211).

SERVES 6~8

50g unsalted butter

2 large Bramley apples, peeled, cored and cut into 10 wedges each

5 Cox's apples, peeled, cored and cut into 8 wedges each

3 tbsp golden caster sugar, mixed with 1 tsp mixed spice

1 quantity of suet pastry (see page 11)

150g blackberries

1 free-range egg, lightly beaten, to glaze

1 tbsp golden caster sugar, mixed with ½ tsp ground cinnamon, for sprinkling

Scrumping fruit, especially apples, from someone else's trees isn't considered as bad as, say, shoplifting, but adults still disapprove. Meanies! Maybe they need to read *The Selfish Giant* . . .

plumble

Mulled wine and plums make an irresistible combination in a crumble. This is a great dish to have up your sleeve when friends or family come round with a bagful of ripe and juicy plums.

Peel the zest from the tangerines with a vegetable peeler, leaving the white pith behind. Squeeze out the juice. Put the juice and strips of zest in a pan with the wine, sugar and spices, bring to the boil and simmer until reduced by half.

Preheat the oven to 180°C/350°F/gas mark 4. Put the plums into a large pan and strain the red wine on to them, discarding the spices. Bring to a simmer, then cover and cook gently for about 10 minutes, until the plums just start to break up a little. Remove them with a slotted spoon and set aside. Boil the liquid until reduced by half again to make a sticky syrup.

For the crumble topping, put all the ingredients into a bowl and rub together with your fingertips until the mixture resembles large breadcrumbs.

Divide the plums between 10 cups (don't use your best china!), pour about a tablespoon of syrup over each one and scatter over the crumble mixture. Place on a baking sheet and bake for 15–20 minutes, until lightly browned. Serve with ice cream or custard (see page 211) and any leftover plum juices.

SERVES 10

2 tangerines

1 bottle of red wine

300g soft brown sugar

6 cloves

a piece of cassia bark
or a cinnamon stick

2 star anise

10 allspice berries

a thumb-sized piece of fresh ginger,
roughly sliced

1 vanilla pod, slit open lengthwise

1.5kg plums, stoned and quartered

For the crumble topping
300g plain flour

200g rolled oats

150g caster sugar

250g lightly salted butter,
cut into cubes

nice plums!

winter

winter

Winter is the perfect season to get baking. Warm kitchen, comfort food, and probably the biggest culinary event of the year – Christmas. Which in our households takes the form of a five-day eat-a-thon. Every year a new 'must have' dish seems to appear alongside the old favourites, resulting in an ever-growing festival of food.

This week of feasting is closely followed by the biggest party of the year – New Year's Eve. Why not have a Victorian theme? The Victorians were a rather hedonistic lot (contrary to their prudish image), with the gentlemen of the time enjoying burlesque dance troupes and clubs such as the Beefsteak or the Savage. A Victorian strongman costume never fails to impress.

SEASONAL HIGHLIGHTS

Vegetables
Brussels sprouts, celeriac, celery, chicory, endive, Jerusalem artichokes, kale and cavolo nero, leeks, parsnips, red and white cabbages, swede, turnips, winter greens

Fruit
apples, pears, quinces, rhubarb (forced)

Wild plants
(greens, flowers, fruit, fungi, nuts)
chestnuts

Game
goose, grouse, hare, mallard, partridge, snipe, venison, woodcock, wood pigeon

Fish and shellfish
cod, mackerel, sea bass, squid, whiting, clams, cockles, crab, crayfish, langoustines, lobster, mussels, oysters

clapshot pie

Shepherds pie! Schmepherds pie! You won't look back with this recipe.

Heat the oil in a large pan, add the vegetables and cook until lightly coloured. Add the mince and fry over a medium heat, stirring frequently, for 5–10 minutes, until it is cooked through. Stir in the flour, then gradually stir in the stock. Season with soy sauce and black pepper, bring to a simmer and cook for 5–10 minutes, until slightly thickened. Strain through a sieve, reserving the liquid, then put the mince mixture into an ovenproof dish and set aside.

Preheat the oven to 180°C/350°F/gas mark 4. For the clapshot, cook the swede and potatoes in separate pans of boiling salted water until tender, then drain thoroughly. Tip them both into the same pan, mash with the butter and milk and season to taste – these vegetables are good with plenty of black pepper.

Spread the mash over the mince. Sprinkle with the grated cheese and place in the oven for 35–40 minutes, until the cheese is golden and bubbling. Sprinkle with the crispy shallots. Reheat the reserved cooking liquid from the mince, then taste and adjust the seasoning if necessary. Serve with the clapshot.

SERVES 8

2 tbsp vegetable oil

1 large onion, finely diced

2 large carrots, peeled and finely diced

2 celery sticks, finely diced

800g minced lamb

3 tbsp plain flour

800ml lamb or chicken stock

soy sauce, to taste

125g Cheddar cheese, grated

50g crispy shallots

freshly ground black pepper

For the clapshot

800g swede, peeled and diced

800g potatoes, peeled and diced

125g butter

125g milk

sea salt and black pepper

酥脆青蔥

Crispy shallots are a revelation! They bring a new angle to the texture party. Get hold of them in Chinese stores; they can also be found lurking near the baked beans in some supermarkets.

stargazing quail pie

Inspired by the classic Cornish stargazey pie, we've replaced pilchards with quails and added lots of Middle Eastern promise.

SERVES 4

First make the filling. Heat the oil in a pan, add the onion and garlic and cook over a very low heat for 15–20 minutes, until translucent and golden. Transfer to a bowl, add the pine nuts, sultanas, spices, thyme, lemon zest and juice and mix well. Season with salt and pepper.

Heat a deep pan over a medium-high heat, add about a tablespoon of water and put in the spinach. Cover and cook for 30 seconds or so, until wilted, then transfer to a colander. Cool slightly, then squeeze out as much liquid as possible. Add the spinach to the spice mix with the Greek yoghurt. Set the filling aside.

Heat the olive oil and butter in a frying pan large enough to hold the quails. Season the birds with salt and pepper and fry for about 5 minutes, until golden all over. Remove from the heat and stuff loosely with some of the filling. Preheat the oven to 180°C/350°F/gas mark 4.

Put the remaining filling in a fairly deep, medium-sized ovenproof dish and make 4 spaces in it to hold the quails. Put them in so their legs are sticking up, pushing the filling around them if necessary to keep them upright.

Roll out the pastry on a lightly floured surface to about 3mm thick. Put the dish on top and cut round it to make a circle. Remove the dish, cut 4 quail-sized pieces out of the pastry and remove them. Lift up the remaining pastry and fit it round the birds in the dish. Brush with egg and sprinkle liberally with sesame seeds. Bake for 35–40 minutes, until the pastry is golden and the birds are thoroughly cooked. Serve with tabouleh, harissa and Greek yoghurt.

2 tbsp olive oil

20g butter

4 quails

150g puff pastry

1 free-range egg, lightly beaten, to glaze

sesame seeds, to decorate

For the filling

2 tbsp olive oil

1 large onion, very finely chopped

1 large garlic clove, very finely chopped

100g pine nuts, lightly toasted

150g sultanas

1 tbsp cumin seeds, lightly toasted in a dry frying pan

1 tsp fennel seeds, lightly toasted in a dry frying pan

1 tbsp ras-al-hanout

a small bunch of thyme, leaves picked and chopped

juice and grated zest of 1 lemon

450g baby spinach

2 tbsp extra-thick Greek yoghurt

sea salt and black pepper

bristol palace's 'who ate all the ox cheek & mushroom' pies

Cheeks are so underrated. They take lots of slow cooking but are melt-in-the-mouth – just ask Bristol Palace, the team we sponsor.

SERVES 6

Soak the porcini in 150ml hot water for 15 minutes, then drain, reserving the water. Preheat the oven to 130°C/275°F/gas mark ¾. Season the flour and toss the cheeks in it, reserving any leftover flour. Heat the oil and half the butter in a large pan and brown the meat in it in batches, transferring it to a casserole as it is done. Add the stout, stock, 1.5 litres of water, and half the quantities of porcini, tomato purée, thyme and mustard to the casserole. Bring to a simmer, then cover, place in the oven and cook for 4 hours, topping the mixture up with stock or water if it starts to look dry.

Melt half the remaining butter in a frying pan, put in the shallots and sugar and cook gently for 10 minutes, then add the garlic and cook for a further 5 minutes, until golden. Remove from the pan and set aside. Melt the remaining butter in the pan and fry the portobello mushrooms until tender. Season and add to the shallots.

Remove the cheeks from the casserole. Slice off any fat and tough membrane and dice the meat. Strain the liquid into a saucepan and add the wine, rosemary, the remaining tomato purée, thyme, mustard and porcini, plus 100ml of the porcini water. Bring to the boil, skim well and add the meat and any leftover flour. Simmer for 5 minutes, then stir in the shallots and mushrooms. Season and leave to cool.

Preheat the oven to 180°C/350°F/gas mark 4. Roll out the shortcrust pastry on a lightly floured surface to about 3mm thick and use to line 6 individual pie dishes. Spoon in the filling and brush the pastry edges with a little beaten egg. Roll out the suet pastry to about 5mm thick, cut out lids to fit the pie dishes and lay them on top of the pies. Trim off any excess and press the edges together to seal. Brush all over with beaten egg and make a small hole in the centre of each pie. Leave to stand for 10 minutes, then place in the oven and bake for 25–30 minutes, until golden. Serve with creamy mash (see page 208) and gravy.

25g dried porcini mushrooms

30g plain flour

1.5kg ox cheeks, fat left on

1 tbsp olive oil

50g butter

400ml Bristol Beer Factory Milk Stout (or other stout)

500ml beef stock

1 tbsp tomato purée

1 tsp chopped thyme

1 tbsp English mustard

150g shallots, finely sliced

1 tsp caster sugar

2 large garlic cloves, finely chopped

250g portobello mushrooms, roughly chopped

400ml good-quality red wine

1 tsp chopped rosemary

1 quantity of shortcrust pastry (see page 10)

1 quantity of suet pastry (see page 11)

1 free-range egg, lightly beaten, to glaze

sea salt and black pepper

'moo-dy blues' steak & stilton pie

Rich and comforting, especially for anyone with the blues and in need of some love. Use Cheddar if you find the thought of Stilton off-putting, as indeed some folk do. We don't want to push our friends and lovers over the edge!

Heat the oil in a large pan, add the vegetables and garlic and cook over a medium heat for about 15 minutes, until golden. Add the beef and cook for about 5 minutes, until sealed all over. Stir in the flour, then add the bay leaves, mustard powder, thyme and tomato purée. Add the red wine and stir well. Pour in the beef stock, bring to a simmer, then cover and cook over a very low heat for about 2 hours, until the beef is tender. Season to taste, then transfer the mixture to a pie dish and leave to cool.

Heat the oven to 180°C/350°F/gas mark 4. Roll out the pastry on a lightly floured surface to about 5mm thick. Crumble the Stilton over the beef filling. Brush the rim of the pie dish with a little of the beaten egg, then lift up the pastry on the rolling pin and use to cover the dish. Trim off the excess pastry and press down all the way round to seal. Brush the pastry with beaten egg, then make slits in the top so you can see the cheese. Bake for about 30 minutes, until the pastry is golden brown. Serve with English mustard mash (see page 208) and steamed cabbage, tossed briefly in a pan with fried bacon lardons.

2 tbsp olive oil

1 onion, chopped

2 celery sticks, chopped

2 carrots, peeled and chopped

1 garlic clove, finely chopped

600g beef skirt, brisket or decent stewing steak, cut into 2.5cm cubes

2 tbsp plain flour

2 bay leaves

1 tbsp English mustard powder

a few sprigs of thyme, leaves picked and chopped

1 tbsp tomato purée

1 large glass of red wine

600ml beef stock

1 quantity of rough puff pastry (see page 10) or 375g puff pastry

200g Stilton cheese, crumbled

1 free-range egg, lightly beaten, to glaze

sea salt and black pepper

rabbit & chorizo pork pie

**Rabbit, chorizo, sherry jelly, raised pie . . .
This will have your competitive foodie friends
crying into their cappuccinos of snail!**

First make the stock. Put the trotters, vegetables, spices and
bay leaves in a saucepan and add enough water to cover.
Bring to a simmer, reduce the heat and cook very gently for
about 2½ hours, skimming off any scum. Strain the stock
into a clean pan, discarding the solids, and add the sherry.
Bring back to the boil and simmer until reduced to about
300ml. Set aside at room temperature for an hour.

For the filling, mix together the rabbit meat, chorizo and
pork, seasoning well with salt and pepper, then stir in
100ml of the sherry stock.

Preheat the oven to 180°C/350°F/gas mark 4. Roll out the
pastry on a lightly floured surface to about 8mm thick,
then cut out one circle about 30cm in diameter and another
11–12cm in diameter. Pile up the filling in the middle of the
large circle and brush the edges of the pastry with beaten
egg. Put the small pastry circle on top of the filling and brush
it all over with egg. Bring up the pastry around the filling
and press it to the pastry lid to seal, then pleat it with your
fingers all the way round so it fits the filling neatly. Brush
the whole thing with egg, making sure the top and sides are
well sealed and smoothing the join. Make a hole about the
size of a 5p coin in the centre of the pastry lid – this is for
pouring in the stock later. Bake for about 2 hours, covering
the pie loosely with foil if it browns too quickly. To test if it's
done, push a skewer into the centre, then draw it out – the tip
should be hot.

Remove the pie from oven, and leave to cool for 10 minutes.
If the remaining stock has thickened to a jelly, warm it
slightly – it should be just liquid, but not hot. Slowly pour
in the stock through the hole in the top of the pie. The stock
will rise to the top; let it settle, then pour in a little more. You
can put your finger in the hole and carefully move the meat
around to create more room if the stock doesn't seem to be
going down. Leave until the pie is completely cold and the
stock has set to jelly. Serve with piccalilli salad (see page 210).

250g rabbit meat, coarsely minced
or chopped

250g cooking chorizo, coarsely
chopped

250g minced pork

1 quantity of hot water crust pastry
(see page 11)

1 free-range egg, lightly beaten,
to glaze

sea salt and black pepper

For the sherry stock

2 pig's trotters

2 celery sticks, roughly chopped

2 carrots, roughly chopped

1 onion, roughly chopped

1 star anise

6 juniper berries

10 peppercorns

2 bay leaves

400ml dry sherry

christmas party games

Human buckaroo

You will need:
❶ **One sleeping friend**
❷ **At least two other players**
❸ **An assortment of everyday objects**
❹ **A camera**

A modern (and mainly drunken) take on the traditional children's game of Buckaroo. This variant requires a group of friends to place objects on to a sleeping target without the target waking or indeed 'bucking'. Any number of objects can be used – get inventive, the stranger the better – and do make sure you have a camera at the ready to capture the moment of realization.

The chocolate game

You will need:
❶ **At least three players**
❷ **One large bar of chocolate
(wrapped in several extra layers of paper)**
❸ **A knife and fork**
❹ **An assortment of clothes –
usually hat, scarf, gloves and coat**
❺ **A die**

The idea of the game is to eat as much of the chocolate as you can. The chocolate bar is placed in the centre of play (usually on a chair or small table) with the items of clothing. Each player takes it in turn to roll the die. The first player to roll a six can start to put the clothes on and then attempt to get into the chocolate bar using the knife and fork. Players continue to roll the die and as soon as another player rolls a six he or she shouts 'Six!' The player in the centre then stops and passes the clothing to his or her successor. Play continues until all the chocolate has been eaten – or players are so exhausted they can no longer participate.

Jumping flame trick

You will need:
❶ **A candle**
❷ **A box of matches**
❸ **Keen observation**

This trick is perfectly suited to the Christmas dinner table, where there are often candles. The 'magician' lights a match from the flame of a candle, then blows out the candle. After a few moments he (or she) holds the lit match a little way above the blown-out wick. Amazingly, the flame from the match jumps down and re-lights it.

The secret of this trick lies in watching the curling plume of smoke as it leaves the extinguished wick. The magician must hold the lit match within the smoke trail and the flame should travel back down the curl of smoke to the wick. Keep your eye on the smoke and you may be able to make the flame 'jump' after a minute or more, or leap as much as a few centimetres.

Wink murder

You will need:
❶ **At least four players**
❷ **Pen and paper to draw lots**

This traditional parlour game, also known as Murder in the Dark, can be played with a minimum of four people, although it's more fun if you can recruit a larger number of willing victims. One person is assigned the role of 'murderer' by drawing lots. The murderer is then able to 'kill' other players by making eye contact and winking at them. The objective is for the murderer to 'kill' as many people as possible without being detected.

caper cod saint jacks

A fish pie that is quick to make ... and foodies will love it. If you are unable to find cod cheeks, don't weep — cod fillet is a tasty and more easily procured substitute.

Preheat the oven to 180°C/350°F/gas mark 4. Put the cod on a baking tray, season well and drizzle with a little olive oil. Place in the oven and bake for 8–10 minutes, until just cooked. Remove from the oven and leave until cool enough to handle.

Mix the fennel, artichokes, parsley, crème fraîche and capers together and season to taste. Add the cod cheeks and stir to coat them in the mixture. Divide between 6 shallow dishes, or scallop shells if you have them.

Roll out the puff pastry thinly on a lightly floured surface to 2mm, cut out 6 rounds slightly larger than the pie dishes or scallop shells and use to cover the pies. Press down the edges of the pastry on the outside of the dishes or shells to seal. Brush with the beaten egg and make a small hole in the centre of each one. Scatter the pastry with fennel seeds. Place the pies in the oven and bake for about 20 minutes, until golden brown. Great with a winter salad (see page 210).

400g cod cheeks, trimmed

a little olive oil

1 small fennel bulb, very finely sliced

100g artichokes preserved in olive oil, drained and finely sliced

a small bunch of parsley, finely shredded

300ml crème fraîche

2 tbsp baby capers

375g puff pastry

1 free-range egg, lightly beaten, to glaze

fennel seeds, to decorate

sea salt and black pepper

6 scallop shells (not vital, but fun)

Cod cheeks are a revelation. They are absolutely delicious tossed in seasoned flour, cooked in hot bubbling butter then finished with capers, lemon and parsley and a grind of black pepper. Serve with crusty bread.

mr jefferson's parmigiana pie

Many of our pies have been developed with our friend, Stinky. His real name is Lincoln Newton Jefferson. One of his school reports once said that 'Lincoln Newton Jefferson will never live up to his name'. In fact, the boy is a culinary genius. He has frightening levels of moral courage and, like Minnie the Moocher, he has a heart as big as a whale!

Preheat the oven to 200°C/400°F/gas mark 6. Spread out the aubergine slices on oiled baking sheets, then drizzle with olive oil and season well. Place in the oven and roast for 15–20 minutes, until they are tender and starting to turn golden. Remove from the oven and set aside.

Next make the tomato sauce. Heat the olive oil in a saucepan, add the garlic and chilli and cook over a gentle heat until the garlic is lightly coloured. Throw in the rosemary, cook for 30 seconds, then stir in the balsamic vinegar. Simmer until it has reduced and starts to smell sweet. Add the tomato passata, season with salt and pepper and bring to a simmer. Cook for 10 minutes, until slightly thickened.

Spread a little of the tomato sauce over the base of an ovenproof dish, add a layer of aubergines, then a light sprinkling of breadcrumbs, followed by a layer of mozzarella. Repeat these layers until all the ingredients are used up, ending with aubergines and a good layer of breadcrumbs. Sprinkle over the grated Parmesan cheese and drizzle with olive oil. Bake at 180°C/350°F/gas mark 4 for 25–30 minutes, until golden brown and bubbling. Serve with a crisp green salad and crusty bread.

SERVES 6

4 large aubergines, cut lengthwise into slices about 5mm thick

olive oil for drizzling

150g breadcrumbs

4 balls of buffalo mozzarella, drained and thinly sliced

50g Parmesan cheese, freshly grated

For the tomato sauce

4 tbsp olive oil

6 garlic cloves, sliced

a pinch of dried chilli flakes

a small bunch of rosemary, leaves picked and chopped

1 tbsp balsamic vinegar

600ml tomato passata

sea salt and black pepper

GOOD
COOKS
NEVER LACK
FRIENDS!

(OLD ADAGE)

cheesy tom's beef hash with homemade baked beans

1kg beef brisket

2 large carrots, peeled and roughly chopped

2 celery sticks, roughly chopped

1 onion, roughly chopped

2 bay leaves

10 peppercorns

enough beef stock to cover (about 2 litres)

sea salt and black pepper

For the topping

1kg potatoes, peeled and cut into chunks

250g butter

5 large onions, sliced

a small bunch of parsley, chopped

200g mature Cheddar cheese, grated

For the baked beans

2 tbsp olive oil

1 onion, finely chopped

2 celery sticks, finely chopped

1 garlic clove, finely chopped

1 tsp dried oregano

2 bay leaves

a pinch of dried chilli flakes

400ml tomato passata

400g can of haricot beans, drained

a pinch of sugar (optional)

Tom Calver is a great bloke, a great cook and handsome to boot. He makes amazing Cheddar (Westcombe), has a lovely wife called Mel, and runs an idyllic farm in Somerset with his parents. Enjoy some of the Calvers' deliciousness by knocking up this recipe.

Put the beef brisket, vegetables, bay leaves and peppercorns into a large pan and add enough beef stock to cover. Bring to a simmer, then cover the pan and cook over a very low heat for about 3 hours, until the beef is very tender. Check from time to time that it is not getting too dry, and top up with water if necessary. Remove the brisket from the pan. Strain the stock (you can keep it to use in other recipes) and discard the vegetables. When the beef is cool enough to handle, shred it roughly and set aside. Preheat the oven to 180°C/350°F/gas mark 4.

For the topping, cook the potatoes in boiling salted water until tender, then drain. Melt the butter in a large frying pan, add the onions and cook for about 15 minutes, until they are tender and golden. Put the potatoes into a large bowl with the parsley and add the onions and their butter. Add the shredded brisket and mix well, then season to taste. Put the mixture into a large ovenproof dish and scatter over the grated cheese. Bake for about 35 minutes, until the topping is golden and lovely.

Meanwhile, prepare the baked beans. Heat the oil in a pan, add the onion, celery and garlic and cook over a medium heat for 5–10 minutes, until the vegetables are translucent and slightly golden. Add the oregano, bay leaves and chilli flakes, followed by the passata and the drained beans. Season with salt and pepper and simmer for about 10 minutes, until the sauce has thickened slightly. Taste and add a little sugar if necessary. Serve the beans with the hash.

the morning after

Hangover cures have been around for as long as people have had one drink too many. One of the earliest recorded remedies comes from Ancient Mesopotamia – the 7,000-year-old recipe recommends a mixture of beans, oleander, licorice, oil and wine. Since then, all kinds of unusual (and frequently disgusting) concoctions have appeared wherever alcohol has been drunk. The Ancient Greeks were famously partial to deep-fried canaries as a cure for a sore head, while their Roman counterparts swore by sheep's lungs and owl eggs. Rabbit-dropping tea was the pick-me-up of choice for cowboys in the American Wild West and deep-fried bull's penis is one traditional recipe in Sicily.

We prefer something a little more palatable. Bananas are a good place to start – they're rich in potassium, one of the nutrients you lose most of when you drink, and high in magnesium, which can help relax pounding blood vessels in your head. If you can't stomach a whole banana, try making a fruit smoothie with it.

Researchers have also shown that amino acids in eggs and bacon can help counter the toxins produced by alcohol in the body, as well as giving neurotransmitters in the brain a bit of a boost. So the full English breakfast might just be the answer – try our pie version of this classic on page 30.

Dehydration is the main culprit in a hangover so try to drink plenty of water after (or during) a heavy night and before going to bed. If you miss the boat on that one, make sure you quaff down loads of water as soon as you wake up.

In our experience, however, the ultimate remedy is a good, old-fashioned 'hair of the dog' – and nothing beats a Bloody Mary. Here's our version:

Ingredients
2 ice cubes
50ml good-quality vodka
25ml sherry
3 twists of freshly ground black pepper
a pinch of Maldon sea salt
a squeeze of lime juice
150ml Clamato
150ml tomato juice
a dash of Tabasco
a dash of Worcestershire sauce

Shake in a cocktail shaker, strain and serve in a big glass. Add a celery stick and sprinkle with celery salt . . . Drink.

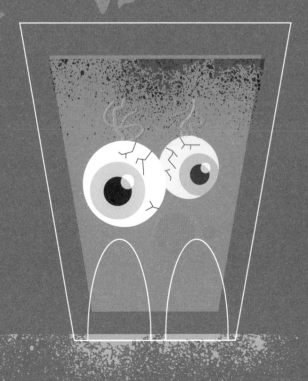

plink
plink

canapies ™

You'd never guess it, but at pieminister we love to play on words. Sometimes we change names because we don't like the original ones, and here is a textbook example. 'Finger food' sounds gruesome, 'canapés' sound pansy, but canapies sound tasty! This is just one recipe for these irresistible little numbers – you can make a spectacular canapie out of almost every recipe in this book. Get to it.

Mix together all the ingredients for the filling, check the seasoning and set aside. Preheat the oven to 200°C/400°F/ gas mark 6.

Roll out the shortcrust pastry on a lightly floured surface to about 3mm thick and cut it into circles to fit a 12-hole bun tray, or muffin tins if you want deeper pies. Press the pastry into the tins. Fill with the salmon mixture and brush the edges of the pastry with beaten egg.

Roll out the puff pastry to about 3mm thick and cut out circles to make lids. Use to cover the pies, pressing the edges together to seal. To give a decorative finish, like the one in the picture, press the edge of each pie down with a teaspoon handle, then use the side of the handle and your thumb to crimp it. Brush with beaten egg, then make a small hole in the centre of each pie and top with a lemon triangle. Sprinkle with a little sea salt and coarsely ground black pepper. Leave to stand for about 10 minutes. Place the pies in the oven and bake for 15–20 minutes, until golden brown. They go exceptionally well with a Bloody Mary (see page 187).

SERVES 12

½ quantity of shortcrust pastry (see page 10)

200g puff pastry

1 free-range egg, lightly beaten

12 tiny triangles of lemon, tossed with a little olive oil, to decorate

For the filling

200g hot-smoked salmon, flaked

300ml crème fraîche

a small bunch of dill, finely chopped

a small bunch of tarragon, finely chopped

grated zest of 1 lemon

1 red chilli, finely chopped

sea salt and black pepper

christingle pies

We made up these pies a few years ago for our herbivore friends so they would have something a little more inspired for Christmas dinner than a nut roast and sprouts. They have been a real hit for us and, what's more, even hardened carnivores have fallen for their charms.

Heat the oil and butter in a large pan, add the vegetables and cook over a medium heat for about 15 minutes, until they are a good golden brown. Stir in the rosemary and sage and cook for a couple of minutes longer. Add the sherry and let it bubble until reduced by about half. Add the cream, bring back to a simmer and reduce by half again. Remove from the heat and stir in the mustard and cranberry jelly, followed by the parsley. Stir in the Cheddar, then season to taste with salt and pepper. Leave to cool.

Preheat the oven to 180°C/350°F/gas mark 4. Roll out the shortcrust pastry on a lightly floured surface to about 3mm thick. Cut in half and use to line 2 individual pie dishes, pushing it well into the corners of each one and letting it overhang the sides slightly. Divide the filling between the dishes and brush the pastry edges with egg.

Roll out the suet pastry to about 3mm thick and cut out 2 pieces to fit the tops of the dishes. Cover the pies with the pastry, pressing the edges to the shortcrust pastry to seal. Brush with beaten egg, make a small hole in the centre of each one and decorate with the pastry trimmings, brushing them with egg too. Leave to stand for 10 minutes or so. Bake the pies for about 35 minutes, until well browned. Great served with all the non-meaty Christmas trimmings.

2 tbsp olive oil

25g butter

2 large shallots, chopped

3 large parsnips, peeled and chopped

200g celeriac, peeled and chopped

a small bunch of rosemary, leaves picked and chopped

10 sage leaves, chopped

100ml dry sherry

300ml double cream

1 tsp English mustard

1 tbsp cranberry jelly

a small bunch of parsley, chopped

200g mature Cheddar cheese, crumbled or grated

½ quantity of shortcrust pastry (see page 10)

½ quantity of suet pastry (see page 11)

1 free-range egg, lightly beaten, to glaze

sea salt and black pepper

leftovers pie

We like leftovers, which is lucky because we were brought up on them. Not sure where they came from, though, as leftovers is all we ate! Perfect for Boxing Day, this recipe will neatly clear you out of turkey, the king of leftovers. If you have used other fowl, such as goose, pheasant or swan (if you're reading this, your Majesty), then feel free to pie them up.

First make the sauce. Melt the butter in a saucepan, stir in the flour and cook gently for 2–3 minutes. Gradually stir in the hot stock, then bring to the boil, stirring all the time. Simmer for a few minutes, pour in the cream and bring back to the boil. Simmer for a few minutes longer, until you have a smooth sauce. Stir in the mustard, then taste and season as necessary – if you have used ham stock you probably won't need any salt.

Roughly shred the leftover turkey and dice the ham. Put the meat in a large pie dish with the vegetables and the stuffing, if using, pour over the sauce and mix well so everything is coated in the sauce. Push a pie funnel into the centre of the mixture, if you have one.

Preheat the oven to 180°C/350°F/gas mark 4. Roll out the pastry on a lightly floured surface to about 3mm thick. Brush the edges of the pie dish with a little of the beaten egg. Lift up the pastry on the rolling pin and use to cover the pie. Trim off the excess pastry, leaving a little overhanging the sides, then tuck under to give a neat edge. Press down with your thumb all around the edge to seal.

Brush the pastry with beaten egg and sprinkle with black pepper. If you haven't put a pie funnel in the pie, make a couple of small slits in the centre of the pastry with a sharp knife. Place in the oven and bake for about 40 minutes, until the pastry is golden brown and the filling is piping hot. If you have any cranberry sauce and gravy left over, you could mix them together, heat thoroughly and serve with the pie.

SERVES 6

500g leftover cooked turkey

300g leftover cooked ham

about 300g leftover cooked vegetables

about 300g leftover stuffing, if you have it

1 quantity of rough puff pastry (see page 10) or 500g puff pastry

1 free-range egg, lightly beaten, to glaze

For the velouté sauce

125g butter

115g plain flour

600ml hot ham stock (or giblet, chicken or turkey stock)

600ml double cream

2 heaped tbsp wholegrain mustard

sea salt and black pepper

deerstalker pies

In northern Italy, cotechino and lentils are the dish to have at New Year in order to bring you prosperity and luck. We've supercharged your chances of obtaining both by adding venison.

Heat the oil in a large casserole, add the vegetables, garlic and bacon and sweat until slightly softened. Add the chilli and thyme and cook for a minute longer. Raise the heat, add the venison and cook until lightly browned all over. Stir in the crumbled cotechino sausage and cook for 2–3 minutes.

Pour in the red wine and simmer until reduced by half. Add the lentils, spices, bay leaf, tomato passata, stock and a little salt and pepper and bring to a simmer. Cover and cook gently for 1–1½ hours, until the meat is tender. Taste and adjust the seasoning. Remove from the heat and leave to cool.

Preheat the oven to 180°C/350°F/gas mark 4. Roll out the shortcrust pastry to about 3mm thick. Take 6 pie dishes about 12cm in diameter and place them upside down on the pastry, then cut round each one, leaving a margin of 7–8cm. The pastry circles need to be large enough to line the pie dishes with a little overlap. Roll out the suet pastry to 3mm thick and cut out 6 circles to fit the tops of the dishes. Line the dishes with the shortcrust pastry, pushing it well into the bottom of each one and letting it overhang the sides slightly. Spoon in the venison mixture, then brush the pastry edges with beaten egg. Cover the pies with the suet pastry circles, pressing the edges to the shortcrust pastry to seal.

Brush with beaten egg, make a small hole in the centre of each one and decorate with the pastry trimmings, brushing them with egg too. Leave to stand for 10 minutes or so. Bake the pies for about 35 minutes, until well browned.

felice anno nuovo! (that's italian for happy new year)

4 tbsp olive oil

2 large shallots, roughly chopped

2 carrots, peeled and roughly chopped

1 celery stick, roughly chopped

1 small head of celeriac, peeled and roughly chopped

2 garlic cloves, sliced

100g streaky bacon, diced

1 red chilli, sliced

a few sprigs of thyme, leaves picked and chopped

500g venison, cut into 3–4cm cubes

250g cotechino sausage, skin removed, crumbled (Italian sausages also work if you cannot get hold of cotechino)

1 glass of red wine

100g Puy lentils

3–4 juniper berries, lightly crushed

1 tsp ground allspice

1 cinnamon stick

1 bay leaf

3 tbsp tomato passata

600ml beef stock

1 quantity of shortcrust pastry (see page 10)

1 quantity of suet pastry (see page 11)

1 free-range egg, lightly beaten, to glaze

sea salt and black pepper

new year's resolutions

We all know about the classic resolutions you vow to stick to as the bells chime . . . no more week-night drinking, at least five portions of fruit a day, no more stress about the little things at work, more quality time with the family. But let's be honest, within the week, you've resorted to a glass of wine with your supper ('I deserve it after the week I'm having!') and the chocolate biscuit tin has been restocked ('Just in case I get a sugar low!').

So we thought we would give you a list of resolutions you can stick to – whatever your circumstances. They are guilt-free and designed to give you the fun-filled, hedonistic January you have always dreamed of. (Well, almost.)

❶ Try to make someone laugh at least once a day. It costs you nothing but is priceless.

❷ Shop locally at least once a week – do your bit to keep your high street thriving. You'll miss it when it's gone!

❸ Ask your local greengrocer to deliver a box of fruit to your office every Monday and eat it during the week. Share the cost with your colleagues.

❹ Start a Friday lunch club at work. All go to the pub together and have a meal.

❺ Start meat-free Mondays. You will discover some great veggie food, save money and you will be helping the environment.

❻ Book a holiday by the end of January. Even if it's just a weekend camping trip, it's great to have something to look forward to.

❼ Eat dinner with your family or a loved one at the table at least once a week. And talk to each other!

❽ Grow something you can eat this year. For veg growing tips, see pages 28–29.

❾ Learn more about where your food comes from – it will allow you to make more informed choices about which food you buy and when.

❿ Sing out loud in the shower – it makes you feel good and makes your family or housemates laugh.

New Year's resolutions

Make a list ☑

caro's apple & blueberry canoodle

A hug and a squeeze of a pudding, to be baked for one's true love.

Put the apples, lemon zest and juice, sugar and spice in a pan and bring to a low simmer. Cover and cook gently for 15–20 minutes, until the apples are very tender but still hold their shape. Remove from the heat, stir in the blueberries and leave to cool.

Preheat the oven to 180°C/350°F/gas mark 4. Place a sheet of filo pastry on a damp tea towel, brush with melted butter and sprinkle with nuts. Add another sheet of filo, butter it and sprinkle with more nuts. Repeat with the remaining filo, butter and nuts to give a stack of filo sheets (reserve a few nuts to decorate).

Spread the apple filling along one short edge of the pastry, taking it not quite to the edges. Roll the pastry around the filling, using the tea towel to help you roll and tucking in the pastry at the sides once or twice as you go. Turn it so that the seam is underneath and brush all over with melted butter.

Place on a buttered baking sheet and bake for 25–30 minutes, until golden. Brush with melted butter, sprinkle with the remaining nuts and dust with the cinnamon sugar. Serve warm or at room temperature, with cream, custard or ice cream (see page 211).

4 large cooking apples, peeled, cored and chopped

juice and grated zest of 2 lemons

100g soft brown sugar

1 tsp ground mixed spice

200g blueberries

5 sheets of filo pastry

125g unsalted butter, melted

50g chopped toasted hazelnuts

1 tbsp golden caster sugar mixed with ½ tsp ground cinnamon, for dusting (or use icing sugar)

mega mince pie

Does what it says on the tin — it's mega, it's mincy and very pie! A good alternative to Christmas pudding.

SERVES 6~8

Put all the ingredients for the mincemeat except the suet into a large, heavy-based pan and bring to a low simmer. Cover and cook gently, stirring occasionally, for 15–20 minutes, until the apples are tender but still hold their shape. Add the suet and cook for 2–3 minutes longer. Remove from the heat and leave to cool.

Preheat the oven to 180°C/350°F/gas mark 4. Roll out the shortcrust pastry on a lightly floured surface to about 3mm thick and use to line a 25cm loose-bottomed tart tin, trimming off the excess pastry. Fill with the mincemeat, spreading it so the top is level. Brush the edges of the pastry with a little beaten egg.

Roll out the suet pastry to about 3mm thick and use to cover the pie. Cut a star template out of cardboard, put it on top of the pastry and cut around it, removing the pastry in between so you have just a pastry star on top of the pie. Gently press the points of the star on to the edges of the shortcrust to seal. Brush the star with beaten egg, then leave the pie to stand for 10 minutes.

Place in the oven and bake for 40–50 minutes, until the pastry is golden brown. Mix the mascarpone with the icing sugar and brandy and serve with the pie (brandy butter goes well with it too).

½ quantity of shortcrust pastry (see page 10)

1 free-range egg, lightly beaten, to glaze

½ quantity of suet pastry (see page 11)

icing sugar for dusting

For the mincemeat

6 cooking apples, peeled, cored and roughly chopped

juice and grated zest of 3 mandarins or clementines

150g sultanas

150g raisins

200g candied mixed peel, finely chopped

1 tsp ground mixed spice

1 tsp ground allspice

½ tsp ground mace

¼ tsp grated nutmeg

200g soft brown sugar

4 tbsp brandy

200g suet

For the brandy mascarpone

500g mascarpone cheese

1 tbsp icing sugar

1 tbsp brandy, or to taste

it's chriiiiissstmassss!

the hedonist pie

AKA Sailor Jerry's hedonistic chocolate tart, this is about as excessively rich and naughty as food can get. It certainly proves that Oscar Wilde was right when he said, 'Moderation is a fatal thing. Nothing succeeds like excess.'

Preheat the oven to 160°C/320°F/gas mark 3. Roll out the pastry on a lightly floured surface to about 3mm thick and use to line a 23cm loose-bottomed tart tin. Line the pastry with baking parchment and fill with rice or baking beans. Bake blind for about 20 minutes, until the pastry is lightly coloured. Take out of the oven (but don't turn the oven off) and leave to cool, then remove the paper and beans.

Meanwhile, toast the hazelnuts: spread them out in a baking tin, place in the oven and leave for 5 minutes until lightly browned. Tip them into a plastic bag and bash with a rolling pin until lightly crushed. Set aside.

To make the filling, put the butter and chocolate in a bowl and place over a pan of gently simmering water, making sure the water isn't touching the base of the bowl. Leave until melted. Whisk the eggs, cocoa powder and sugar together until well combined and slightly thickened. Remove the chocolate mixture from the heat, pour in the cream and mix together gently. Add the clementine or mandarin zest and the hazelnuts. Pour this mixture into the eggs and sugar and mix well. Finally mix in the rum. Pour into the pastry case, place in the oven and bake for 20–25 minutes or until the filling is almost set; it should still have a very slight wobble in the middle when you nudge the tin.

Remove the pie from the oven and leave for at least 2 hours before serving. Best eaten with large dollops of clotted cream, and with a dram or two of Sailor Jerry rum on the rocks.

SERVES 8

½ quantity of sweet pastry
(see page 12)

50g roasted hazelnuts

150g slightly salted butter, diced

150g dark chocolate, broken up

3 free-range eggs

1½ tbsp cocoa powder

100g caster sugar

150ml double cream

grated zest of 1 clementine or
mandarin

50ml dark rum, such as Sailor Jerry

clotted cream (or crème fraîche),
to serve

accompaniments

mashed spuds, the pieminister way

Everyone has their own way of making mash. There is the good stuff and the bad stuff, but this one works. It's a basic but super-creamy mash to which we tend to add other bits to match our pies (and moods). Mustard mash, for example, is great with rich, beefy pies.

Serves 6
1.4kg floury potatoes, such as Desiree or Maris Piper
1 tbsp salt
150g butter
150ml double cream

Wash the spuds, peel them and wash again. Cut them into roughly equal pieces so they all cook at the same speed. Put into a pan, add enough water just to cover, then add the salt. Bring to the boil, reduce the heat and simmer until tender: they are ready when they fall off the blade easily if stabbed with a knife – or just take one out, cut a bit off and taste it. Pour off as much water as you can before putting the potatoes in a colander; the less water to drain, the better. Leave in the colander for a few minutes to make sure all the remaining moisture steams off, then give them a shake just to make sure.

Meanwhile, warm the butter and cream together in the potato pan. Once the mixture is hot, push the fully drained spuds back into the pan through a mouli-légumes (a big, spinny masher that works amazingly well) or a potato ricer (which is an oversized garlic press, basically) and stir briskly with a wooden spoon to add to the creaminess. Alternatively, dropping the potatoes into the cream and butter and mashing away with a potato masher until smooth does the trick. Taste and add more seasoning if necessary.

flavoured mashes

Some ingredients are best added directly to the warmed cream and butter, to ensure even mixing. Others, such as cheese, need to be stirred in after mashing so that you don't get a homogenous mix, and herbs are added right at the end. All the quantities given below are a rough guide – adjust to suit your taste.

pre-mash additions

Roast garlic – roast a whole bulb of garlic in a moderate oven until tender. Pop out the flesh from the garlic skin and add to the cream and butter mix.

Smoked paprika – add 2 tsp smoked paprika to the cream and butter mix.

Mustard – add 1 tbsp wholegrain, English or Dijon mustard to the cream and butter mix.

Horseradish – add 1 tbsp creamed horseradish to the cream and butter mix.

Black pepper – add a good pinch of freshly ground black pepper to the cream and butter mix.

post-mash additions

Cheddar – grate in 150g Cheddar cheese after mashing and stir it through.

Champ – finely chop 1 large bunch of spring onions and stir them through.

Chive – finely chop a bunch of chives and stir them in at the end.

Boursin – crumble in a Boursin cheese at the end and stir it through.

Black pudding – fry 200g good-quality black pudding in a little oil, then crumble it into the mash.

minty MPs (minty mushy peas)

A pieminister classic and a key component of our famous mothership meal: pie, mustard mash, minty MPs, red wine gravy, grated Cheddar cheese and crispy shallots.

Serves 4–6

300g mushy peas (from a tin)
150g fresh or thawed frozen peas
1 tbsp mint sauce, or to taste

Mix everything together in a pan and heat gently. Yum.

pea and carrot velouté

Admittedly a little 1980s *cordon bleu* but 62 million French people can't be wrong.

Serves 4

40g butter
200g carrots, cut into pea-sized dice
1½ tbsp plain flour
300ml dry cider
100ml chicken stock
a small bunch of thyme, leaves chopped
2 bay leaves
200g peas
sea salt and black pepper

Melt the butter in a pan, add the carrots and sweat for about 5 minutes, until softened. Stir in the flour, then gradually stir in the cider and stock. Add the thyme and bay leaves, season and simmer for about 5 minutes, then stir in the peas and cook for a couple of minutes longer.

braised red cabbage

A majestic side, best made in advance for the flavours to find one another.

Serves 4

75g butter
5 shallots, sliced
3 garlic cloves, chopped
½ red cabbage, core removed, sliced
4 tbsp cider vinegar
300ml dry cider
4 tbsp demerara sugar
3 star anise
1 tsp ground cinnamon

2 well-flavoured dessert apples, such as Cox's, peeled, cored and roughly chopped (optional)
sea salt and black pepper

Melt the butter in a pan, add the shallots and cook gently for 4–5 minutes, until lightly coloured. Stir in the garlic and red cabbage, then add the vinegar, cider, sugar, star anise and cinnamon. Bring to a simmer and cook over a medium heat for 20–25 minutes, until the butter and sugar start to caramelize the cabbage and the liquid reduces to a glaze. Season with salt and pepper, add the apples and cook for about 5 minutes, until they are just tender but still holding their shape.

herb salad

Serve this Arabic-style salad as soon as possible after preparation to keep everything crisp and fresh.

Serves 6

a bunch of flat-leaf parsley
a bunch of mint
a bunch of dill
a bunch of coriander
1 large cucumber, peeled, deseeded and diced
4 shallots, finely sliced
1 tsp sumac (optional)
juice of ½ lemon, or to taste
2 tbsp extra virgin olive oil
sea salt and black pepper

Briefly soak all the herbs in ice-cold water to remove any grit. Shake the herbs, then pat dry with a clean tea towel. Finely chop the leaves, put them in a bowl with all the other ingredients and toss well. Adjust the seasoning if necessary and serve.

sweet chilli crème fraîche

A good dip for summery pies and also great with trashy (yet delicious) food such as crisps, burgers and fish fingers.

Serves 4–6

150ml crème fraîche
1 tablespoon sweet chilli sauce
juice of ½ lime

Put everything into a bowl and mix well.

winter salad

Winter salad with a pie. Really? Yes, really! It's good to keep challenging yourself.

Serves 6

1 large raw beetroot, grated
1 small celeriac, peeled and grated
1 fennel bulb, finely sliced
4 shallots, finely sliced
2 bunches of watercress, tough stalks
  removed
2 tbsp extra virgin olive oil
juice of 1 lemon
a big blob of creamed horseradish
sea salt and black pepper

Put all the ingredients in a bowl and toss together well. Do not make too far in advance or the watercress will wilt.

red cabbage slaw

Crunchy, delectable and goes with almost everything.

Serves 6

½ red cabbage, core removed, finely sliced
2 carrots, peeled and grated
a small bunch of chives, finely chopped
1 tbsp sweet chilli sauce
1 tsp sesame seeds
a hearty splash of balsamic vinegar
a few good slugs of extra virgin olive oil
sea salt and black pepper

Mix everything together. Simples.

mango and pineapple salsa

This salsa will transport you and your pies to sunny climes.

Serves 4–6

1 cucumber, peeled, halved lengthwise,
  deseeded and diced
1 mango, peeled, stoned and diced
1 red onion, finely diced
$^1/_3$ pineapple, diced
a small bunch of coriander, chopped
a small handful of radishes, sliced
1 tbsp sweet chilli sauce, or to taste
juice of 1 lime

Mix together all the ingredients. That's it.

piccalilli salad

This was inspired by Fergus Henderson of St John restaurant and *Nose to Tail Eating* fame. A British institution.

Serves 4–6

500g French beans
1 tsp English mustard
1 tsp wholegrain mustard
2 garlic cloves, crushed
1 tsp caster sugar
a good splash of sherry vinegar
1 tsp ground turmeric (optional)
200ml extra virgin olive oil
1 cauliflower, divided into florets
1 cucumber, halved lengthwise, deseeded,
  then cut into strips about 4cm long
1 red onion, finely sliced
1 tbsp baby capers
sea salt and black pepper

Cook the French beans in boiling salted water until just tender; drain and refresh in cold water. Mix together the mustards, garlic, sugar, vinegar and turmeric, if using, then gradually whisk in the oil. Season to taste. Put all the vegetables in a bowl, add the capers and toss with the dressing.

beetroot pickle

This goes so well with sausage rolls, pork pies and on top of cheese on toast, no less.

Serves 6

1 tbsp groundnut or vegetable oil
1 tsp fennel seeds
6 cloves
1 tsp mustard seeds
1 tsp coriander seeds
1 dried red chilli, finely shredded
400g raw beetroot, peeled and diced
100ml sherry vinegar
2 tbsp golden granulated sugar

Heat the oil in a frying pan, add the spices and cook until they start to pop. Add the beetroot, vinegar and sugar and cook over a fairly high heat, stirring frequently, until the liquid has reduced to a syrup and the beetroot is just tender but still has some bite. Season to taste, then leave to cool.

colonel custard's fragrant custard

Intelligent imperialist custard with a monocle!

Serves 4–6

1 vanilla pod
2 strips of lemon zest, removed using
  a vegetable peeler
a small knob of fresh ginger, finely sliced
4 cardamom pods, lightly bruised
275ml double cream
3 large free-range egg yolks (or, if you're
  feeling flush, procure 2 goose egg yolks
  instead for extra richness and indulgence)
25g golden caster sugar

Slit the vanilla pod open lengthwise with a sharp knife and scoop out the seeds with the point of the knife. Place the pod and seeds in a small, heavy-based saucepan, along with the lemon zest, ginger, cardamom and cream. Heat gently to just below simmering point, then remove from the heat and set aside to infuse the cream with the aromatics.

Beat the egg yolks and sugar together in a bowl until pale. Strain the hot cream to remove the aromatics, then gradually pour it on to the egg mix, stirring constantly. Rinse out the saucepan and return the custard to it. Place over a low heat and cook, stirring with a wooden spoon, until the custard is thick enough to coat the back of the spoon; don't let it boil or it will separate. Pour the custard through a sieve into a jug or bowl. Serve hot or cold – if you are leaving it to cool, press a piece of clingfilm over the surface to prevent a skin forming.

clotted cream ice cream

A real ice-creamy dreamy experience. An ice-cream machine is not strictly necessary but it does help.

Serves 8

10 free-range egg yolks
225g caster sugar
600ml Jersey clotted cream
300ml whole milk

Beat the egg yolks with the sugar until pale. Put the cream and milk in a heavy-based pan and bring to the boil over a medium heat, stirring occasionally. Remove from the heat and gradually pour on to the egg yolk mixture, mixing continuously. Rinse out the pan, pour the mixture back into it and cook over a low heat, stirring constantly with a wooden spoon, until the mixture thickens enough to coat the back of the spoon; don't let it boil or it will separate. Pour through a fine sieve and leave to cool.

If using an ice-cream maker, churn the mixture according to the manufacturer's instructions, then transfer to a plastic box or a bowl, cover and store in the freezer until needed. If you don't have an ice-cream maker, pour the mixture into a large container and freeze for about 30 minutes. Remove from the freezer and beat with a whisk or a fork to get air into the mixture and prevent ice crystals forming. Repeat every 20 minutes or so for about 4 hours, until the ice cream is light, fluffy and totally delectable. Transfer to a smaller plastic box or bowl and store in the freezer.

hunter's chicken pie

SERVES 4~6

For the final recipe in this book we decided to get our loyal pie-eaters involved. So many people sent in their own delicious recipes and we had the painful task of deciding which one would best fit in our book. Katie Alcorn's yummy idea for a hunter's pie won the day and hopefully it will be a winner for you too. Thanks, Katie A, you're a real champ.

First make the barbecue relish. Heat the oil in a pan, add the onions and rosemary, then cover and cook gently for about 20 minutes, until the onions are soft but not coloured. Take off the lid, raise the heat a little and cook until any liquid has evaporated and the onions are beginning to colour. Stir in the tomatoes, tomato purée and some salt and pepper and cook for 3–4 minutes, until the tomatoes have broken down. Add the vinegar, sugar and Worcestershire sauce and cook for a few minutes longer, until the relish is thick. Add the lemon juice, then taste and adjust the seasoning. Leave to cool.

Heat the butter in a large, heavy-based frying pan, add the chicken and fry over a medium heat until lightly browned underneath. Turn the chicken over, add the bacon and fry until the bacon is lightly coloured and the chicken is just cooked through. Stir in the flour, then gradually stir in the stock, followed by the cream. Simmer for 2–3 minutes, until slightly thickened, then add the mustard and season to taste. Remove from the heat and leave to cool.

Preheat the oven to 180°C/350°F/gas mark 4. Roll out about two-thirds of the pastry on a lightly floured surface to about 3mm thick and use to line a 23cm pie plate. Add the chicken mixture, then dollop about half the relish randomly over the top. Scatter over the grated cheese. Brush the pastry edges with a little beaten egg.

Roll out the remaining pastry and use to cover the pie, trimming off the excess and pressing the edges together well to seal. Make a couple of holes in the centre to let out steam, then brush all over with beaten egg. Place in the oven and bake for about 30 minutes, until the pastry is well browned. Serve with the remaining relish on the side.

30g butter

500g chicken meat, diced

4 smoked back bacon rashers, chopped

1 tbsp plain flour

150ml chicken stock

150ml double cream

2 tsp wholegrain mustard

1 quantity of rough puff pastry (see page 10) or 500g puff pastry

a good handful of grated Cheddar cheese

1 free-range egg, lightly beaten

sea salt and black pepper

For the barbecue relish

2 tbsp olive oil

4 onions, thinly sliced

a small bunch of rosemary, leaves picked and chopped

2 tomatoes, skinned and finely diced

4 tsp tomato purée

1 tbsp balsamic vinegar

1 tbsp demerara or soft brown sugar

a dash of Worcestershire sauce

a squeeze of lemon juice

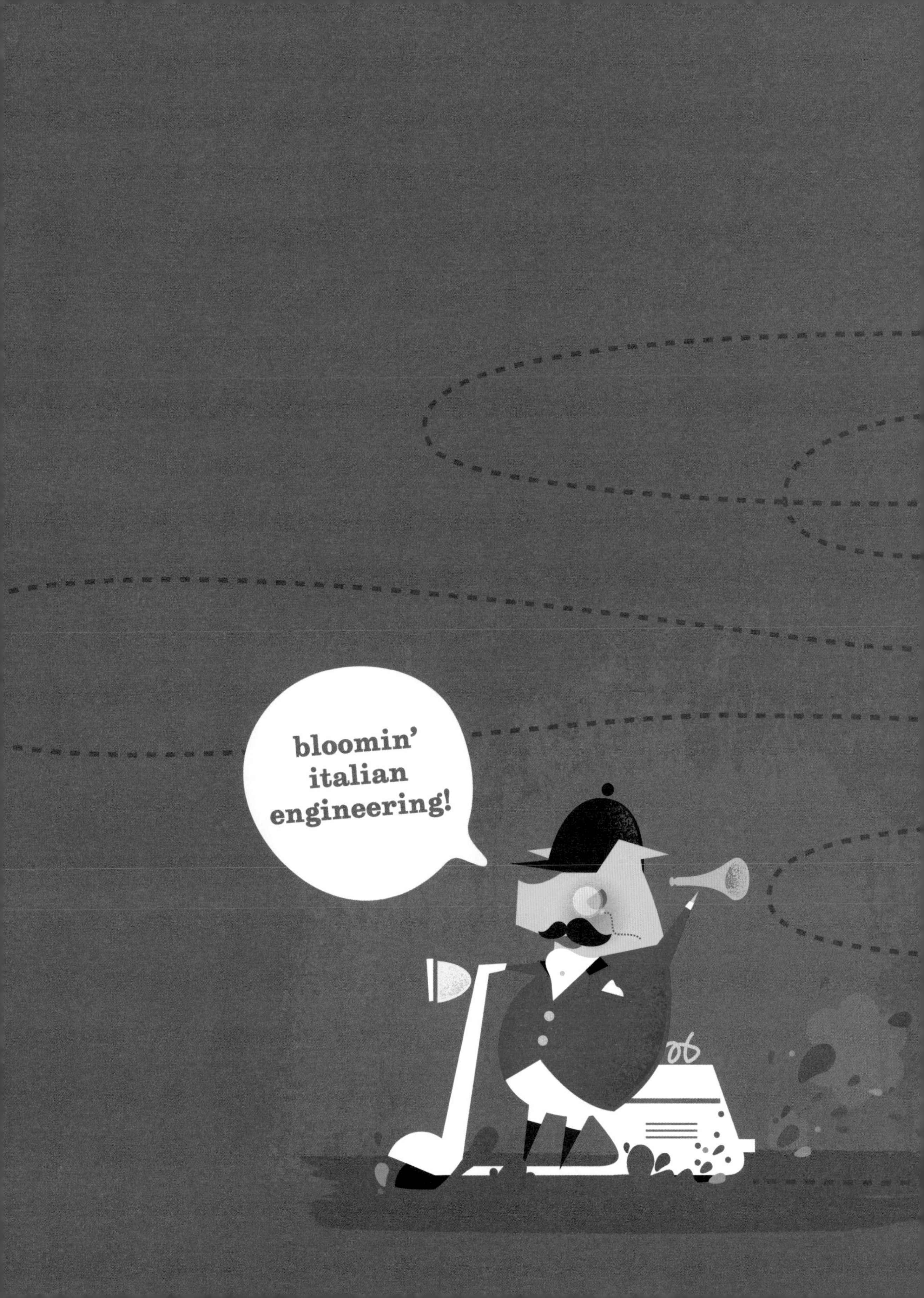
bloomin' italian engineering!

a baker's dozen

The spirit of the pie revolution will continue for as long as our pieminister bakers' hearts and hands keep grafting and crafting.

❶ **Simon**, fearless leader
❷ **Chris**, casserole chef
❸ **Craig**, caretaker
❹ **Evalina**, pie checker
❺ **Wieslava**, packer
❻ **Adam** and **Geneen**, goods out
❼ **Pavo**, trucker
❽ **Rashim**, chief pieman
❾ **Burchill**, blocker
❿ **Fred**, casserole chef
⓫ **John**, pie finisher
⓬ **Keith**, high care boss

index

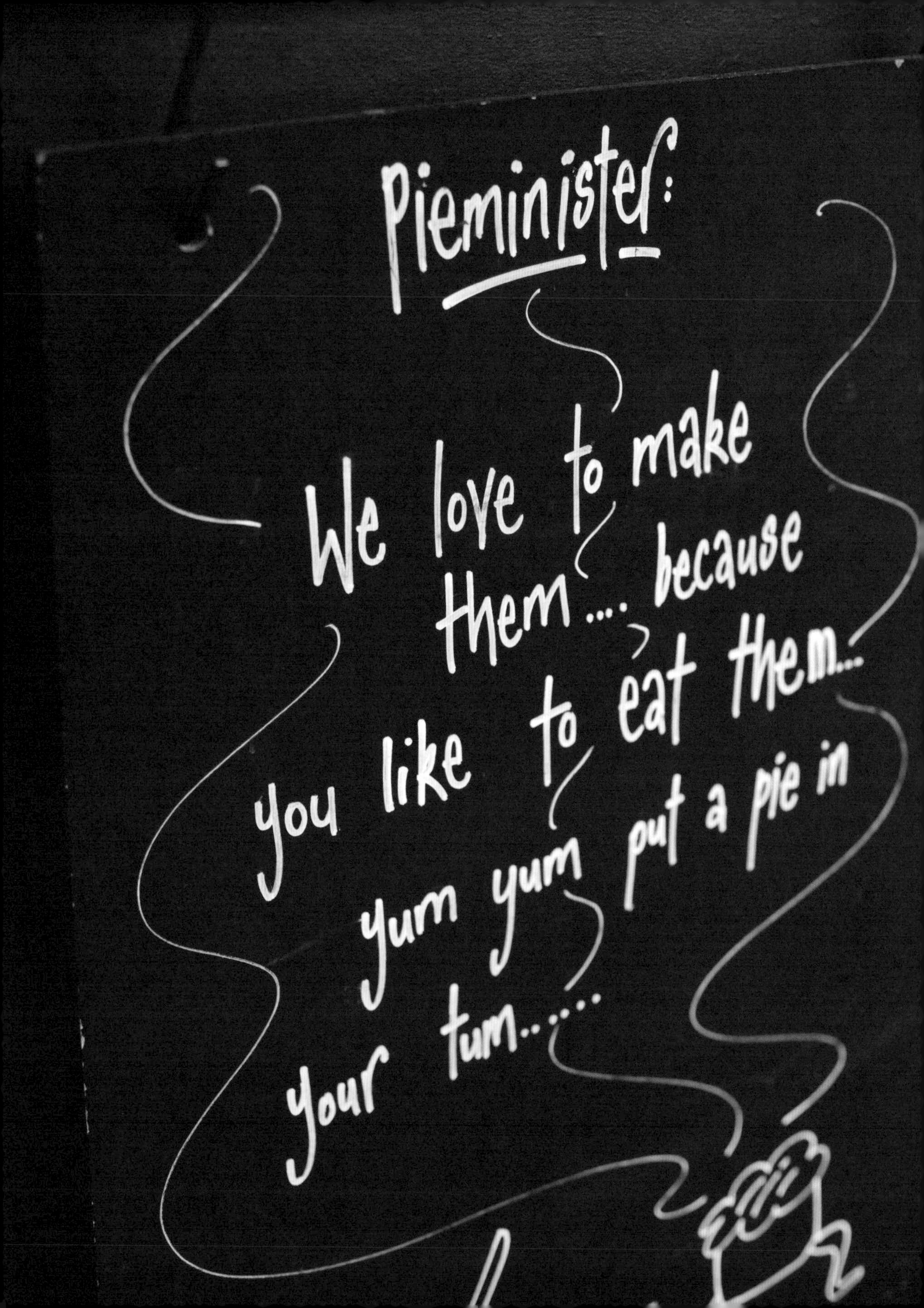
Pieminister:
We love to make them.... because you like to eat them... yum yum put a pie in your tum......

For our mums and dads

Enjoy x

Acknowledgements
Caroline Harris, Clive Wilson, Lincoln 'Stinky' Jefferson,
A-Side Studio, Ryan Thomas, James Bowden, Jane Middleton,
Romany Simon, Jennie Spears, Doug Young and everyone else
at Transworld.

Special thanks to
Caroline Davey at Fat Hen, Tom Calver and family at Westcombe
Dairy, Chris and Gemma Saunders, Orchard Pig, the Raglan Road
revellers, Imogen and Sam Hunt and their wedding guests,
Bristol Palace football team, The Thali Café, Gemma and Tess Bush
for the beach hut, the Pringle family.

And the biggest thank you of all to everyone who has supported us
and ever eaten a pieminister pie . . .

Long live the pie!